Praise for *Agile Project Management with Kanban*

"I have been fortunate to work closely with Eric for many years. In that time he has been one of the most productive, consistent, and efficient engineering leaders at Xbox. His philosophy and approach to software engineering are truly successful."

—Kareem Choudhry, Partner Director of Software Engineering for Xbox

"Eric easily explains why Kanban has proven itself as a useful method for managing and tracking complicated work. Don't expect this book to be an overview, however. Eric channels his deep understanding and experiences using Kanban at Microsoft to help you identify and avoid many of the common difficulties and risks when implementing Kanban."

—Richard Hundhausen, President, Accentient Inc.

"Learning how Xbox uses Kanban on large-scale development of their platform lends real credibility to the validity of the method. Eric Brechner is a hands-on software development management practitioner who tells it like it is—solid, practical, pragmatic advice from someone who does it for a living."

—David J. Anderson, Chairman, Lean Kanban Inc.

"As a software development coach, I continuously search for the perfect reference to pragmatically apply Kanban for continuous software delivery. Finally, my search is over."

—James Waletzky, Partner, Crosslake Technologies

"Kanban has been incredibly effective at helping our team in Xbox manage shifting priorities and requirements in a very demanding environment. The concepts covered in Agile Project Management with Kanban *give us the framework to process our work on a daily basis to give our customers the high-quality results they deserve."*

—Doug Thompson, Principal Program Manager, Xbox Engineering

"An exceptional book for those who want to deliver software with high quality, predictability, and flexibility. Eric's in-depth experience in the software industry has resulted in a realistic book that teaches Kanban in a simple and easy way. It is a must-read for every software professional!"

—Vijay Garg, Senior Program Manager, Xbox Engineering

Agile Project Management with Kanban

ERIC BRECHNER

WITH A CONTRIBUTION FROM JAMES WALETZKY

PUBLISHED BY
Microsoft Press
A Division of Microsoft Corporation
One Microsoft Way
Redmond, Washington 98052-6399

Library of Congress Control Number: 2014951864
ISBN: 978-0-7356-9895-6

Printed and bound in the United States of America.

3   17

Microsoft Press books are available through booksellers and distributors worldwide. If you need support related to this book, email Microsoft Press Book Support at mspinput@microsoft.com. Please tell us what you think of this book at http://www.microsoft.com/learning/booksurvey.

Microsoft and the trademarks listed at http://www.microsoft.com/about/legal/en/us/IntellectualProperty/Trademarks/EN-US.aspx are trademarks of the Microsoft group of companies. All other marks are property of their respective owners.

The example companies, organizations, products, domain names, email addresses, logos, people, places, and events depicted herein are fictitious. No association with any real company, organization, product, domain name, email address, logo, person, place, or event is intended or should be inferred.

This book expresses the author's views and opinions. The information contained in this book is provided without any express, statutory, or implied warranties. Neither the authors, Microsoft Corporation, nor its resellers, or distributors will be held liable for any damages caused or alleged to be caused either directly or indirectly by this book.

Acquisitions Editor: Devon Musgrave
Developmental Editor: Devon Musgrave
Project Editor: Devon Musgrave
Editorial Production: Rob Nance, John Pierce, and Carrie Wicks
Copyeditor: John Pierce
Indexer: Lucie Haskins
Cover: Twist Creative • Seattle

Table of Contents

Chapter 4   Adapting from Waterfall   39

Chapter 5   Evolving from Scrum   57

Chapter 6   Deploying components, apps, and services   71

Introduction

I'm a professional software developer. I've been one for decades (currently with Xbox). I don't get paid to be a certified process geek. I don't get paid to be an evangelical process zealot. I get paid to deliver software that customers love, with high quality, on time, and at low cost.

I develop software in a highly volatile environment, where priorities, requirements, and expectations change daily. I develop software in a highly competitive environ-ment—for market share among products and for compensation among peers. My software development peers inhabit this same world, regardless of where they work or what products they produce.

I'm always looking for advantages over my competition—ways that make my life easier and more productive while also resulting in better products for my customers. When I was at Bank Leumi, Jet Propulsion Laboratory, Graftek, and Silicon Graphics in the 1980s, I focused on what we now refer to as design patterns and unit testing. During the 1990s, while I was at Boeing and starting out at Microsoft, my teams and I tried Waterfall milestones and stabilization periods of different durations, T-shirt estimation, asserts, bug jail, continuous integration, and design and code reviews. In the 2000s, the Microsoft teams I managed experimented with Team Software Process, Scrum, code inspection, static analysis, planning poker, pair programming, and test-driven development. Now in the 2010s, I've found continuous deployment, Kanban, and a little nirvana.

Some of the methods I just listed may not be familiar to you. Most of the profes-sional software developers I've known don't like experimenting with how they do their jobs. They find an approach that works for them, usually the one they learn from their first professional software team, and tend to stay with that approach.

Trying different methodologies is painful and has an initial drain on productivity, but it has enabled my teams to outperform those of my peers. My teams are significantly smaller than other teams doing similar work, yet they produce significantly more value at significantly higher quality in the same or less time. That's not because I've filled my teams with mythical developers who work twenty times faster than anyone else. (I've got good people, but they aren't mythical.) My teams simply get more value out of every hour.

You could experiment with all the methods I've tried, but that's time-consuming and tedious. Though my teams and I have learned from every experiment, not all have been of equal value. My current and former teams still use design patterns, unit testing, continuous integration, design and code reviews, static analysis, planning poker, pair programming, test-driven development, and continuous deployment to varying degrees. However, it was Scrum that had the biggest impact on team productivity and quality—that is, until we switched to Kanban four years ago. With Kanban, for the first time in my long career, I can honestly say that every minute of work my teams do adds value for customers to our products. No time or effort is wasted, and quality is assured.

This book is about how you can duplicate my success with your teams. I've done all the experimenting. I've taken all the missteps. I've culled what's important, and I've laid it out for you in plain language and straightforward steps so that you get just the benefits. Don't let your peers read this book, make use of Kanban, and start making you look antiquated. Take the easy steps I describe and start producing better software that customers love—with high quality, on time, and at low cost.

Who should read this book

This book is for practicing or aspiring software development professionals. You might have started creating software in the 1960s or are just now graduating from college. You could be part of an established software company or an IT organization within a larger company, or you could be a do-it-yourself app or web developer. You might be a software analyst, project manager, program manager, developer, tester, project lead, or development manager. So long as you are a serious practitioner of software development, you will find this book enlightening and invaluable.

This book provides pragmatic and prescriptive step-by-step instructions on how to produce the most value for your customers, with the highest quality at the lowest cost in the least amount of time. I've included diagrams, tables, charts, worksheets, rude Q & A sections, and troubleshooting sections to clarify concepts and guide you toward success. This book also has chapters especially for people who want to adapt from traditional Waterfall methods or evolve from Scrum.

This book might not be for you if . . .

Although the last chapter, "Further resources and beyond," covers the basic theory behind Kanban and other techniques, this book might not be for you if you're look-ing for a deep reference. Students, academics, and consultants might prefer a different text for in-depth analysis of theory and practice. I suggest several such texts in the last chapter.

Organization of this book

The book follows the progression that a feature team (3–10 people) might experience when learning Kanban:

- Chapter 1, "Getting management consent," covers approaches and steps for gaining consent from management to use Kanban (a necessary condition before you start). This chapter includes an open letter to your manager with a sample proposal.

- Chapter 2, "Kanban quick-start guide," can get you going with Kanban within a few days, provided you have an existing backlog of work. The chapter also includes a troubleshooting section.

- Chapter 3, "Hitting deadlines," helps team members fill and order their backlog as well as estimate how long their project will take and how many resources they'll need.

- Chapter 4, "Adapting from Waterfall," and Chapter 5, "Evolving from Scrum," are for teams that currently use traditional Waterfall or Scrum. These chapters summarize the argument for using Kanban, provide the steps to adapt or evolve to Kanban, and answer the questions a team might have. These chapters and their rude Q & A sections are based on my direct experience with introducing traditional Waterfall and Scrum teams to Kanban.

- Chapter 6, "Deploying components, apps, and services," focuses on delivering the value you produce with Kanban to customers—everything from continuous integration to continuous deployment.

- Chapter 7, "Using Kanban within large organizations," is for teams that use Kanban within large projects of hundreds or thousands of engineers, including how to fit in and report up.

- Chapter 8, "Sustained engineering," is a special contribution from James Waletzky about how to apply Kanban to perform postrelease software maintenance.

- Chapter 9, "Further resources and beyond," provides an overview of the theoretical underpinnings of Kanban and covers how you can improve beyond the practices described in the previous chapters. This chapter provides resources for those who want to continue learning and evolving.

Acknowledgments

I'll start by congratulating Microsoft Press on its thirtieth anniversary. It was at the anniversary party in Redmond that Devon Musgrave approached me about writing this book. Many thanks to Devon for his suggestion and for championing the book's publication. I'm also deeply indebted to my editor, John Pierce, who did wonders to the readability and consistency of my words.

This book had six reviewers: David Anderson, Corey Ladas, Richard Hundhausen, James Waletzky, Doug Thompson, and Vijay Garg. Doug and Vijay currently work on two of my teams and use Kanban every day. Their feedback was essential to the clarity and accuracy of the text and its examples. James Waletzky is a passionate practitioner of Agile. We've worked together in the past, and his candor and critique have guided my writing for years. James, in his awesomeness, also supplied the chapter on sustained engineering (Chapter 8). Rich joined this project late but provided tremendous suggestions and a tight connection back to the Agile Project Management series. In all, I believe you can't produce worthwhile designs, code, or commentary without thoughtful expert review. To the extent that this book is worthwhile, it is due to my exceptional reviewers.

I want to especially recognize David Anderson and Corey Ladas. David has been an industry leader in project-management techniques throughout his career. He is the originator of the Kanban Method for evolutionary improvement. David speaks and trains professionals around the world. David has always been generous with his time and insights ever since we first collaborated at Microsoft years ago. David's contributions to this book's accuracy, framing, and language are essential and extensive. Even with all his traveling, David found substantial time to carefully review this work, for which I am immensely grateful.

Corey Ladas's influence on my thinking and career cannot be overstated. Corey introduced me to Scrum, Agile, axiomatic design, TRIZ, House of Quality, and numerous other techniques. In 2007, Corey invited me to Corbis to see the work that he and David Anderson were doing there with Kanban. I was instantly enthralled. Although it would take me a few years to try it myself, I immediately shared the work with as many peers as would listen. Corey is a deep thinker, who consistently challenges the status quo. He is fearless and unflinching. Corey can be tough and defiant, but he is always honest and insightful. I am delighted to call him my friend. Corey was the inspiration for this book.

Finally, I'd like to thank my past managers (Curt Steeb, Boyd Multerer, and Kareem Choudhry) for making Xbox such a great place to work, all my team members over the years who embraced experimentation and shared in my success, and, most of all, my wife, Karen, and my sons, Alex and Peter, for making me so very happy.

Downloads: Sample files

I've provided a couple of sample files, which you can download from the following page:

http://aka.ms/pmwithkanban/files

The first file is a sample of a letter and proposal you can provide to your management to gain consent to use Kanban. The second is an Excel workbook with every sample spreadsheet shown in the book, including those to calculate work-in-progress (WIP) limits, estimate completion dates, and even chart productivity and quality over time.

Follow the instructions on the page to download the files.

System requirements

The files provided online are in the Office Open XML format. The basic requirement for using the files is to have an Excel Viewer and Word Viewer installed on your computer.

You can download the Excel viewer from *http://www.microsoft.com/en-us/download/details.aspx?id=10*.

You can download the Word view from *http://www.microsoft.com/en-us/download/details.aspx?id=4*.

Errata, updates, & book support

We've made every effort to ensure the accuracy of this book and its companion content. You can access updates to this book—in the form of a list of submitted errata and their related corrections—at:

http://aka.ms/pmwithkanban/errata

If you discover an error that is not already listed, please submit it to us at the same page.

If you need additional support, email Microsoft Press Book Support at *mspinput@microsoft.com*.

Please note that product support for Microsoft software and hardware is not offered through the previous addresses. For help with Microsoft software or hardware, go to *http://support.microsoft.com*.

Free ebooks from Microsoft Press

From technical overviews to in-depth information on special topics, the free ebooks from Microsoft Press cover a wide range of topics. These ebooks are available in PDF, EPUB, and Mobi for Kindle formats, ready for you to download at:

http://aka.ms/mspressfree

Check back often to see what is new!

We want to hear from you

At Microsoft Press, your satisfaction is our top priority, and your feedback our most valuable asset. Please tell us what you think of this book at:

http://aka.ms/tellpress

We know you're busy, so we've kept it short with just a few questions. Your answers go directly to the editors at Microsoft Press. (No personal information will be requested.) Thanks in advance for your input!

Stay in touch

Let's keep the conversation going! We're on Twitter: *http://twitter.com/MicrosoftPress*

CHAPTER 1

Getting management consent

This book describes how you can manage software projects with great efficiency, predictability, and simplicity using Kanban. Kanban helps you deliver value to your customers faster than Waterfall, Scrum, or just about any other project-management method. It helps you deliver that value with high quality, on time, and on budget, yet it will still fail miserably without the consent of management.

Before you engage in any kind of change, even one as effective as Kanban, you must gain consent from your management. Why? Because employees tend to do what they are told to do—until, that is, those employees realize that they are actually rewarded for doing something else. The people who tell employees what to do are managers. The people who determine employee rewards are managers. Change only succeeds if managers say, "Yes, you should do this," and later reward employees who do it.

Thus, for you and your team to successfully adopt Kanban, you must first convince your management to support it, or at least to not obstruct it and not penalize team members for using it. Even if you are a manager yourself, you still must ensure that your management chain won't oppose Kanban.

Convincing management to make a change, even a good change, can be difficult. A proven approach is to present a proposal that briefly outlines the problem, the solution, the risks with mitigations, measures of success or failure, and a plan for going forward.

For your convenience, I provide a sample proposal in this chapter, in the form of an open letter to your manager. (You can download an editable electronic copy. See the book's introduction for details.) If your manager approves, you can move forward with confidence. If your manager does not approve, even after you address his or her concerns, you should either stop reading and shelve this book or find a new manager. Good luck!

The topics covered are:

An open letter to your manager
Moving forward
Checklist

An open letter to your manager

Dear Sir or Madam,

Our team would like to use Kanban to manage its project work. This proposal lays out the need for this change, why Kanban was selected as a solution, the risks involved and suggested mitigations, and a plan to roll out the change. We look forward to your feedback to this proposal and to enacting the plan once we've addressed any concerns you may have.

Problem

We currently spend significant time doing work that's unrelated to delivering value to our customers.

- We attend an excessive number of meetings about planning and process.

- Problems fester for weeks or months before they are noticed, analyzed, and corrected.

- Careless team members are rewarded for pure speed, encouraging them to create costly bugs and submit incomplete work.

- Quality goes unchecked for weeks or months, which builds up an extensive amount of rework.

- Schedules slip as requirements change and work is reprioritized, which forces more meetings about planning and process and wastes the effort spent on abandoned work.

In the end, our products are delivered late with less functionality and lower quality at higher cost. We used to just accept this outcome because we've always worked this way. However, we now feel we've found a simple and effective solution.

Solution

Kanban is a simple project-management technique that's based on Toyota's just-in-time scheduling mechanism. Using Kanban to manage our project work will allow us to focus all our time and energy on delivering value to our customers.

- Kanban has planning meetings only on demand and no special meetings about process.

- Kanban visualizes project workflow, spotlights bottlenecks the day they occur, and forces team members to immediately resolve the issue or swarm to fix it.

- Kanban prevents careless team members from prematurely designating work as complete.

- Kanban enforces clear quality bars at each step, driving quality upstream.

- Kanban minimizes work in progress, freeing teams to adjust daily to new priorities and requirements with little sunk cost and allowing a team to deliver on time.

Kanban isn't a magic bullet. It won't fix every problem. What it can do is simplify our project management; reduce time lost to meetings, bottlenecks, and rework; better govern our product quality; and make our throughput of customer value smoother, faster, and more predictable.

As with any work change, our team will need a few weeks to adjust to Kanban and a few months to master it. However, we'll all enjoy the benefits—delivering on time with greater functionality and higher quality at lower cost.

Risks

Any change has risks. We list the ones for Kanban along with our planned mitigations.

Risk	Mitigation
Current work could be disrupted as the team acclimates to the new approach.	Adopt Kanban at the start of a new project or milestone.
Some team members could object to the change.	Ensure that team leaders and influencers agree to try Kanban for two months.
A lack of experience with the new approach could cause it to fail.	Invest in a Kanban coach, training, or book for all team members.
The team's productivity could drop during the first few weeks of adjustment.	Reduce expectations of output for the first month.
Status and tracking tools may need to be updated.	Have the team's project manager enter status information daily into the existing tracking tools.
Issues with dependencies and requirements changes could disrupt adoption.	Kanban is inherently good at dealing with scheduling disruptions, so dependency issues and requirements changes will serve well as practice.

Although an initial drop in productivity is expected during the first few weeks (which occurs with any change), the subsequent increases in productivity should quickly recover the lost output.

Plan

Here is an outline of our plan of action, divided into four phases:

Phase	Activities	Duration
1	<ul><li>Brief team leaders and influencers on Kanban (in progress)</li><li>Gain agreement on a two-month trial period</li><li>Communicate adoption plan to team one month in advance</li><li>Provide team with access to Kanban online resources and books</li><li>Utilize experienced coach to answer early questions</li><li>Create baseline of productivity and bug metrics</li></ul>	1 month
2	<ul><li>Train team on Kanban with consultant or team expert</li><li>Collect and organize backlog of work</li><li>Document current steps used to produce value for customers</li><li>Construct progress signboard on wall near team's location</li><li>Determine work-in-progress (WIP) limits</li><li>Establish completion criteria for each step</li></ul>	2 weeks

Phase	Activities	Duration
3	• Run daily standup meetings • Enter status information daily into existing tracking tools • Track productivity and bug metrics • Utilize consultant or team expert to answer team questions • Adjust WIP limits and completion criteria as needed • Reduce expectations of output during this period	1 month
4	• Run daily standup meetings • Enter status information daily into the existing tracking tools • Track productivity and bug metrics • Celebrate performance improvements	Ongoing

Each phase is contingent upon a successful prior phase. Success is measured by completion of each phase's activities and the continued engagement of the team. Overall success is measured by improvement of productivity and bug metrics over the baseline set in the first phase.

We look forward to your feedback to this proposal and to enacting the plan after we've addressed any concerns you may have.

Sincerely,

A team passionate about delivering the greatest value to its customers

Moving forward

Some managers will support the initiative of your team and approve your proposal with few reservations. For them, tracking productivity and bug metrics as your team improves will provide all the positive feedback they need to stand by their decision.

Some managers will be more skeptical and ask for a deeper review. These managers often need to experience Kanban for themselves to remove the mystery, understand the source of productivity and quality gains, and gain confidence in the approach that only personal experience provides. Fortunately, Kanban simulations are available that deliver hands-on practice with the approach and demonstrate how and why it works. It's worth bringing in an experienced Kanban coach to run the simulation and answer your manager's questions. Coaches often have programs that specifically target management concerns.

After your manager's concerns are addressed, you can move forward with the plan described in the letter and detailed in the chapters that follow. For Waterfall and Scrum teams, I have included specific chapters that illustrate how to smooth the adoption of Kanban.

Inside Xbox

When my teams switched to Kanban, I didn't need management permission. As an Xbox development manager, I have the discretion to specify the methods my teams use. However, my teams did need to report progress on features and bugs using the Xbox-wide tracking system.

(We first used a Microsoft internal system, Product Studio, then switched to Visual Studio Team Foundation Server (TFS), and now use Visual Studio Online.) In Chapter 7, "Using Kanban within large organizations," I talk about how to fit Kanban into a big project seamlessly.

I first used Kanban with some of my Scrum teams that worked on web services. I had described Kanban to all my teams and asked whether any would be interested in trying it. Two teams were, and they quickly adapted their work cadence for continuous delivery. Both teams liked Kanban and said they wouldn't go back to Scrum. Both also quickly landed on many of the specific recommendations you'll read about in the coming chapters.

Eight months after I introduced my teams to Kanban, a reorg moved me to a new Xbox group. I had to build much of the new group from scratch, hiring engineers from around Microsoft who were mostly experienced with Waterfall. Since we had no established practices, I simply stated that my teams used Kanban. The Waterfall engineers took to it quickly and were free to adjust Kanban to their needs, so long as they followed the key principles I outline in this book. I capture many of their adjustments in the "Troubleshooting" section in Chapter 2, "Kanban quick-start guide."

Checklist

Here's a checklist of actions to take when gaining management consent for using Kanban:

- ❏ Ask management for consent to use Kanban.
- ❏ Update the proposal language, risks, and plan as needed.
- ❏ Send the proposal to your management.
- ❏ Provide your management with a review of Kanban and with hands-on experience with Kanban as needed.
- ❏ Address any concerns your management raises.
- ❏ Create a baseline of productivity and bug metrics.
- ❏ Execute your plan of action, tracking your improvements in productivity and bug metrics.

CHAPTER 2

Kanban quick-start guide

Kanban provides a simple approach to delivering high-quality value to your customers, on time and on budget. If you already have a set of work items to do and a team ready to do them (as most teams do), use this chapter to get started right away. For those who don't yet have a set of work items or who need to put a team in place, Chapter 3, "Hitting deadlines," describes how to plan your project and staff your team.

The quick-start steps for using Kanban to complete your work backlog are:

Step 1: Capture your team's high-level routine
Step 2: Redecorate your wall
Step 3: Set limits on chaos
Step 4: Define done
Step 5: Run your daily standup
Troubleshooting
Checklist

Step 1: Capture your team's high-level routine

Team members do many kinds of work:

- Discuss the product with partners, teammates, and customers.

- Write and answer email, and engage in relevant social media.

- Find, evaluate, and fix bugs and operational issues (tickets).

- Track feedback.

- Produce improvements to products and infrastructure.

While all this work is important, Kanban focuses primarily on the last and most intrinsic item: producing improvements to products and infrastructure.

There are exceptions that Kanban can also manage, such as the following:

- Preparing for a major presentation.

- Writing proposals or major design documents, or rolling out major changes.

- Fixing a particularly complex bug or operational issue.

- Designing a response to particularly important feedback.

I'll treat these exceptions just as I treat producing improvements (more details in this chapter's "Troubleshooting" section). For now, let's focus on product and infrastructure improvements.

You probably already follow a high-level routine for producing improvements. Here's the one my feature teams (3–10 people) use:

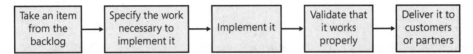

Teams that use very formal methods (perhaps for compliance) or that do in-depth design may use multiple steps to specify a work item. Teams that have complex procedures or standards may use multiple steps to implement or validate a work item. Please write down the steps familiar to your team.

Here are a few guidelines that will help you keep your routine simple:

- **Include only the steps that your team does**   Leave out the steps that occur before items reach your team (such as high-level planning or specification done by other teams) and the steps that take place after items are delivered to customers and partners. You could combine teams and include those steps, but we're keeping things simple for this quick-start guide.

- **If two sequential steps are usually done by the same person, combine those steps**   Again, you want to keep things simple at first. If the developer for an item also usually writes unit tests, implements the code, and drives the code review, just call those three consecutive steps "Implement." Once your work is flowing smoothly, you may want to reexamine each small step to further improve quality and throughput. Chapter 9, "Further resources and beyond" has details.

- **When in doubt, use the steps that I use for my teams**   These steps are fairly common: specify, implement, validate, and deliver.

Step 2: Redecorate your wall

Now that you've captured the steps in your team's high-level routine, you need to post the steps on a signboard close to where your team resides. Your team members will use this signboard to visualize progress and attach note cards to it to track their work. (Kanban means "signboard" in Japanese, but that's not a perfect translation. At Toyota, it means "signal card"—the note cards that track and control work. Another translation of Kanban, from Chinese, is *looking at the board*—thus referring to the daily standup meeting. Since these three elements are essential to Kanban, it's a fitting, versatile name.)

You can hold the note cards in place on a whiteboard or wall by using sticky notes, tape, or magnets or attach them to a corkboard by using pushpins. One of my Xbox teams used magnets taped to the backs of cutouts of their Xbox Live avatars.

Having a signboard close to where your team resides brings up two interesting questions:

- **Why not track your work using only online tools?**   Visualizing workflow is one of Kanban's core principles. Without engaging with workflow in a visceral manner, team members won't recognize and resolve issues as quickly. Manipulating note cards on a signboard is more engaging, faster, and simpler than doing so electronically. (For large organizations, your team's project manager can quickly transfer daily status to electronic tracking tools.)

- **Should your team sit together near the signboard?**   Teams typically work faster when team members sit in close proximity, which enables quicker, easier, and more spontaneous communication. Team members need not sit in a "team room" or in cubicles—offices in a shared hallway work just as well in my experience. Having the signboard nearby is convenient and promotes a sense of identity ("our board in our area"). Kanban can still work well for distributed teams through a virtual signboard online, but if you're given the choice, sitting in close proximity near a physical signboard is better.

After choosing a location for your signboard, it's time to construct two columns for each step, plus a double-width column on the left for the work backlog. The columns for each step should be the width of a note card (sticky note or index card). You can use tape or markers to delineate the columns. Here's what your signboard might look like.

Backlog	Specify work	Implement it	Validate it

Looking back at the steps in the high-level routine that my teams use, notice how the first and last steps are treated differently from the middle steps.

- The first step, "Take an item from the backlog," is replaced by a holding area for pending work. Note cards in the backlog are positioned in the order in which you want to work on the items (your team can reorder the cards at any time). The top card is pulled off when the team is ready to work on the next item. Chapter 3 describes how to fill and sort the backlog.

- The middle steps—specifying, implementing, and validating work—are divided into two columns each. The left column of each step holds active note cards (items being specified, implemented, or validated). The right column of each step holds note cards that have completed that step (items that have been specified, implemented, or validated).

- The last step, "Deliver it to customers or partners," isn't shown because that action is typically handled in bulk by a separate process, like integration into the main branch of a big project or a deployment to production of a web service. I have a detailed discussion of the last step in Chapter 6, "Deploying components, apps, and services."

Inside Xbox

Here's an actual early signboard from one of my teams. We became more sophisticated with the work-in-progress (WIP) limits and added a Track column to Implement later in the project. I describe these techniques later in this chapter.

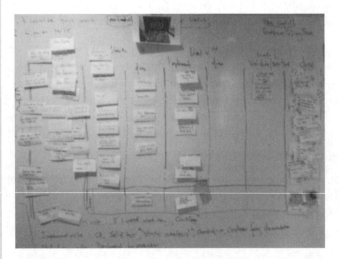

I know this image is blurry and hard to read, but that's to protect confidentiality. At the top left are the foundations of Kanban: "Visualize your work" and "Limit WIP." Top center is a web photo of the maple bar cake the team decided would be its celebratory reward for completing its current project. The leftmost column is the backlog. The next pair of columns is Specify (hidden behind a sticky note) and Done, followed by the pair of Implement columns and the pair of Validate columns. Note the WIP limits (described in the next section) written above each pair of columns. The completion rules for each step are written across the bottom of the board.

Step 3: Set limits on chaos

A large part of project management is limiting the chaos inherent in group work. This step is so important that you can often identify the essence of a project-management methodology by how it limits chaos.

- In a traditional Waterfall approach, chaos is limited by specifying all the work up front, enforcing a formal change-request procedure, and synchronizing work across teams at predetermined milestones.

- In Scrum, chaos is limited by planning time-boxed sprints, withholding plan changes until the next sprint, and synchronizing with the customer at the end of each sprint.

- In Kanban, chaos is limited by directly limiting the amount of work in progress (WIP)—literally, the number of note cards allowed at each step. Simple, yet effective.

The WIP limits in Kanban serve two essential roles in controlling chaos. First, they limit the amount of work affected by changing priorities, requirements, or designs. This frees your team to respond quickly and abandon little. Second, WIP limits restrict the flow of work to match the pace of the slowest step (also known as the "constraint"). Because you can't possibly complete work faster than your slowest step, pacing the other steps to match it yields the greatest efficiency and highest productivity. (See Chapter 9 for details.)

You want to use the smallest WIP limits that still keep your team fully engaged in delivering value to customers.

- Start with setting the WIP limit for your slowest step to the number of team members doing that step, plus a 50 percent buffer. That always keeps the slowest step busy yet still limits the number of note cards at that step.

- Then use ratios to set the WIP limits for the other steps so that their throughput matches the slowest step.

- The result is starting values that you can continually adjust as needed to maximize throughput.

Here's a worksheet with values from one of my old Xbox teams. (You can download an online Excel spreadsheet with the formulas.)

	A	B	C	D	E
1	**Determine WIP Limits**		Fill in cells with yellow highlight		
2					
3	Step	Specify	Implement	Validate	
4	A: Average rate per month per person	6	2	3	
5	B: Slowest rate (minimum A column)		2		
6	C: Number of people assigned to step B		3		
7	D: Throughput of step B (B * C)		6		
8	E: People needed to match B's throughput (D / A)	1	3	2	
9	F: WIP limits (E * 1½ rounded up)	2	5	3	

For the team in this example:

- **A** On average, each analyst can specify roughly six items per month, each developer can implement roughly two items per month, and each tester can validate roughly three items per month. (Since you're using ratios here, you could use per week or per day if that's easier.)

- **B** Implementing was the slowest step (two items per month per person).

- **C** The team had three developers implementing items from the backlog.

- **D** The throughput was six items per month (2 * 3).

- **E** Dividing that throughput by the average rates for each step gives you the people needed for each step to match six items per month (one analyst, three developers, and two testers).

- **F** Adding 50 percent to those people totals and rounding up gives you each step's WIP limit (2 for Specify, 5 for Implement, and 3 for Validate).

The WIP limits from the worksheet are fine starting values. The limits can be adjusted at any time to maximize team output and agility. This chapter's "Troubleshooting" section describes when and how to adjust WIP limits for the best outcomes.

It's handy to write the WIP limits on your signboard next to each step, like this:

Backlog	Specify (2)	Implement (5)	Validate (3)

Notice how the WIP limit applies to the total number of active and done cards for each step, except for the last step, which has a limited number of active cards but an unlimited number of done cards. (When items are through validation, they are completely done and basically off the board.)

Inside Xbox

At Microsoft, a team's project manager is also its business analyst. We call this role *program manager* (PM). While using one person for both roles might be efficient, it can cause problems if the PM is weak in one area. For large projects (100+ people), the two roles are broken up, with a specialized PM, called a *release manager*, taking on the project-management responsibilities, and feature-team PMs acting mostly as analysts, but who are also responsible for reporting their team's status to the release manager. PM is a tricky role at Microsoft—good PMs are highly valued.

My current teams don't have testers. Developers, automation, or partners validate improvements before they are used by larger customer audiences, basically running a DevOps model (see Chapter 9, "Further resources and beyond," for details on DevOps). We still have a Validate step because that is real work that must be tracked for each item, even though many of the people performing that step might not be on our team. The more you use Kanban, the more you focus on the smooth flow of work than on getting caught up in the people assigned. That turns out to be good for teamwork, efficiency, and continuously delivering customer value.

Step 4: Define done

Kanban regulates quality through a deceptively simple mechanism. Before a note card is moved from the left to the right column of a step, the work on that item must pass certain rules—your definition of "done" for that step (also known as the *pull criteria*). The use of two columns per step in Kanban may seem excessive, but it makes all the difference.

- Items in a step's Done column count toward that step's WIP limit (except for the last step). Remember, you want to match throughput with the slowest step. Thus, if implementation is taking a long time, you could have two items in the Specify step's Done column and not be allowed to specify any more work. That's good. You shouldn't overload implementation, and you should probably be helping to unblock implementation. More about that in this chapter's "Troubleshooting" section.

- Kanban distinguishes between finishing one step and starting the next. Of course, those are always two different things. However, signboards used for Scrum or other daily standup meetings typically move an item to the next step on the board as soon as it's done, thus losing the important distinction between items ready for the next step and items actively in the next step.

- Separating the completion of one step from the initiation of the next decouples the steps. This frees you to have rules that define what it means to be done with each step, regardless of what the next step happens to be.

With the steps decoupled, your team needs to define "done" for each step. I strongly recommend that you define this criteria together as a team, with everyone committing to follow the definitions. Here are examples from another of my Xbox teams (you might have noticed the rules at the bottom of their signboard shown earlier).

- **Specify done rule**   All items broken down into tasks that can be finished in less than a week each, and quick specs completed for each item.

- **Implement done rule**   Code is reviewed and unit tested, the static analysis is clean, the code is checked in, acceptance tests pass, and the customer-facing documentation is complete.

- **Validate done rule**   The work is deployed to production and tried by a significant subset of real customers. All issues found are resolved.

These rules come with a few best practices:

- The first step, Specify in my example, often includes breaking down backlog items into similarly sized short tasks, each with its own new note card. (For example, visiting Disneyland could be broken into seeing Adventureland, Frontierland, Fantasyland, and Tomorrowland.) The WIP limit for the Specify step refers to the original backlog items. You can think of the smaller items as being grouped within that step. Upon leaving the step, the smaller items are considered separate (each short task counts toward the implementation WIP limit). This breakdown does impact throughput, so you may need to adjust your WIP limits over time (details in this chapter's "Troubleshooting" section).

- Before someone moves a note card from left to right in a step, a team member should check that the done rules are met. It's these agreed-upon rules that drive quality upstream at every step and prevent lazy or careless team members from taking credit for incomplete work that responsible team members must finish and fix later. The rules work only when team members hold each other accountable for following them.

- Posting the rules at the bottom of your signboard reminds team members to apply them and provides a central place to discuss the rules should the team decide to change them.

Step 5: Run your daily standup

Now that you've defined what being done means, your team is ready to use Kanban. With a loaded backlog, no planning meetings are necessary. There are no milestones, no sprints, and no retrospectives. Kanban flows continuously, so long as there is work to do.

Naturally, you can still bring the team together at any time for design reviews, demos, customer reviews, and discussions about product and process improvements. However, the only meetings Kanban typically has are daily standup meetings at the team signboard.

Any team member can run the daily standup. My teams' project managers usually do this because it helps them update Xbox online tracking tools. The one required agenda item is asking whether any team members are blocked or otherwise need assistance, then assigning people (often the project manager) to resolve the issues. Experienced teams can complete the standup in five minutes.

My teams also like to use the daily standup to learn what other members are doing and to celebrate the progress they are making together. This makes the meetings a little longer, but it builds a shared sense of pride and ownership.

For an example of a standup, I'll pretend that the team moves note cards only during the standup (not the most efficient process, but easiest to explain). In reality, any team member moves any card at any time, so long as the move doesn't exceed WIP limits and the done rule is met. Also in reality, my teams are a mix of men and women, but I'll stick to male pronouns by default.

At the start, let's say the signboard looks like this:

There are seven planned items in the backlog. One item is being specified, and one item is done being specified (having been broken down into four smaller items, shown together on the same row). Three items are actively being implemented, and two items are done and ready to be validated.

Finally, three items are actively being validated. There are likely a pile of note cards that are done with validation (the last step), but they don't count toward the last step's WIP limit. (One of my Xbox teams used completed cards to wallpaper a team member's office to surprise him when he returned from vacation.)

At the beginning of the daily standup, the project manager starts at the last step, opening up slots when items are done, and works his way to the left. (Because of WIP limits, items can move to the right only if there's room. Pulling cards from the left to the right is what makes Kanban a "pull" system.)

The project manager points to the last step, Validate, and asks, "Any items done being validated?" Team members say two items are done. Other team members check the Validate done rule with questions such as, "How many customers were involved?" When the team is satisfied, team members happily move the two items to the final Done column—more value delivered to customers!

Backlog			Specify (2)		Implement (5)		Validate (3)		
▢	▢		▢	▢▢▢▢	▢	▢	▢		▢
▢	▢				▢	▢			▢
▢	▢				▢				
	▢								

Because items that are completely done don't count toward the final step's WIP limit, there's room to validate two more items. Team members pull two cards from the Implement step's Done column, decide who will do which work item, and then write their names on the cards they've selected.

> **Key point** Work item assignments are made "just in time." This avoids blocking an item because a previously assigned team member is busy at the time the task is ready. (This chapter's "Troubleshooting" section has more details.)

Backlog			Specify (2)		Implement (5)		Validate (3)		
▢	▢		▢	▢▢▢▢	▢		▢	▢	
▢	▢				▢		▢	▢	
▢	▢				▢		▢		
	▢								

Next the project manager asks whether any implementation items are finished. A team member says that one item is done, and another team members says, "That's right, I did the code review, checked the unit tests and static analysis, and the customer-facing documentation looks good. It's all submitted." A team member moves the completed item to the right side of the Implement step.

Backlog | Specify (2) | Implement (5) | Validate (3)

Two slots are still available for Implement (because two items moved to Validate), so team members pull the top two items from the Specify step's Done column, decide who will do which work item, and then write their names on the cards they've selected.

Backlog | Specify (2) | Implement (5) | Validate (3)

Now the project manager asks the analyst whether he's finished specifying the one active item he has. The analyst thanks team members for their feedback on the quick spec and says the item broke down into three smaller tasks that will each take just a few days. The analyst adds three new cards (for the broken-down tasks, shown together on the same row).

Backlog | Specify (2) | Implement (5) | Validate (3)

The analyst doesn't pull another item from the top of the backlog because the Specify step has reached its WIP limit (two items, each of which has been broken down into tasks awaiting implementation).

The project manager asks whether anyone wants to change the order of the backlog based on new requests or requirements. A short discussion ensues, a new item is added, and two items swap places.

Backlog	Specify (2)	Implement (5)	Validate (3)
□ □	□□	□ □	□ □
□ □	□□□	□	□ □
□ □		□	□
□ □		□	

Finally, the project manager asks whether anyone needs extra help. (Remember, this is the only required question at daily standup. Everything else I've described is done by any team member at any time.) The project manager focuses particularly on implementation because the analyst is blocked until a couple of more items have completed the Implement step. One of the team members mentions a few things that need to be sorted out, and the analyst offers to help.

The daily standup is over, and everyone returns to work. The whole process takes less than 15 minutes. The project manager stays behind to enter the status changes of items into the organization's tracking tools and then starts sorting out the issues raised during standup.

Troubleshooting

The daily standup example went smoothly, with only one hitch (needing to help the implementation effort because no more items could be specified). However, all kinds of things can happen, raising many questions. This section covers a wide variety of common issues. I'll start with the one from the example, "What happens when an intermediate step reaches its WIP limit and all items are done?"

Problem: Blocked because all items in an intermediate step are done

In the example, the analyst was blocked because his step, Specify, had a WIP limit of two, he had completed two items, but the Implement step wasn't ready to take them yet. Here's the signboard:

Backlog	Specify (2)	Implement (5)	Validate (3)
□ □	□□	□ □	□ □
□ □	□□□	□	□
□ □		□	□
□ □		□	

The same thing can happen with any step but the last one (which has an unlimited Done column). What should the analyst do?

- He could specify the next item from the backlog, but doing that isn't helpful; it just creates more work for the team to implement, and the team is already at its implementation limit. The team can't go any faster without help. Yes, the next item in the backlog may eventually need to be specified, but that only hides this issue until later, doesn't help solve the problem, and may even result in work being thrown away if priorities change.

- The best thing for the analyst to do is to help with implementation (the next step). He could implement some items himself. He could help with design or implementation issues. He could do some research or work with partner teams that might make implementation faster.

- If there's no way for the analyst to help with implementation, he can still be productive by getting a head start on customer research, advanced planning, or new tooling. There's always productive work available that doesn't hurt the team.

Problem: Blocked because prior step has no items done

Let's say your signboard looks like this:

Backlog		Specify (2)		Implement (5)		Validate (3)	
☐	☐	☐	☐☐☐☐	☐		☐	☐
☐	☐			☐		☐	
☐	☐			☐			
	☐			☐			
				☐			

The Validate step is ready for a new item (the last step's Done column doesn't count toward its WIP limit). However, the Implement step has no items that are done. The testers doing the Validate step are blocked. What should they do?

Just as when the analyst was blocked, the best thing for the testers to do is to help with implementation (the prior step). They could implement some items, help with design or implementation issues, or work with partner teams to make implementation faster. They could even grab lunch for the development team—whatever is needed.

If there's no way for the testers to help with implementation, they can still be productive by analyzing bugs or usage patterns, running experiments, or improving tooling. There's always productive work available that doesn't hurt the team.

Problem: Step taking longer than usual for an item

While different steps require different amounts of time and effort, each step should ideally take about the same amount of time for each item. That's why the first step often breaks down large items to smaller items of similar size. However, there's always variation, and sometimes one step might take unusually long for a particular item.

If a step for an item seems to be taking a long time, team members should review what's happening.

- Perhaps the person assigned to the item is blocked or needs help.

- Perhaps the item should be broken down further into smaller items.

- Perhaps more design work is needed.

- Perhaps the person assigned to the item is expanding the scope of the item inappropriately.

- Perhaps there are some substantial unresolved bugs.

Regardless of the cause, items should always be moving along at a fairly regular pace. Whatever the problem is, the team should address it quickly. I go into more detail about some specific situations later in this section.

Problem: Constantly getting blocked

If team members or work items often seem to be blocked, your team may need to adjust the Specify step, WIP limits, staff assignments, or other variables. The proper action to take depends on the symptoms.

If the flow through your steps is uneven because items vary substantially in size, be sure that your first step (typically Specify or Breakdown) breaks down items into similarly sized tasks. Team members can review the item breakdown to ensure a reasonably consistent result.

If a step still sways from having plenty of work to no work and back again, increase the step's WIP limit by one (extra buffer to handle the variation).

If a step is slow, and the steps before and after are constantly blocked, you've got a few choices:

- Do a root-cause analysis of why the step is so slow, and then speed it up. That could mean assigning more people to the slow step, improving the tools or specs, giving folks faster computers, or whatever helps fix the problem. (See Chapter 9 for more details.)

- Reduce the WIP limits by one for the steps before and after the slow step. Doing this also frees up time for some team members, who should be assigned to the slow step or to other projects. (The minimum WIP limit is one.)

- If team members assigned to the slow step are idle much of the time, increase the WIP limit of the slow step by one. However, be certain that's the real problem—increasing WIP limits should be a last resort.

If a step is fast and always seems to have a full Done column; reduce the step's WIP limit by one. (The minimum WIP limit is one.) The team members assigned to the fast step should then have additional time to do productive work on other projects.

Problem: Item blocked awaiting external input

Items often get blocked midstream awaiting external review, dependencies, questions, approvals, or other input from outside the team. For my Xbox teams, this happens most often at the Implement step.

To handle the issue, we add a Track column to the middle of the Implement step.

Backlog		Specify (2)		Implement (5)			Validate (3)	
		Active	Done	Active	Track	Done	Active	Done
☐	☐		☐☐☐	☐			☐	
☐	☐			☐				
☐	☐			☐				
☐	☐			☐				

Items are moved to the Track column whenever they are blocked awaiting external input. Tracked items don't count toward the Implement WIP limit. We talk about their status during every daily standup until they are unblocked. When a tracked item is unblocked, it moves back to the Active column as soon as a slot becomes available. The logic is that any item already in Implement has higher priority than the next item from Specify. (I talk about other ways to handle late or unstable dependencies in Chapter 7, "Using Kanban within large organizations.")

Occasionally, it becomes apparent that an item will be blocked indefinitely. We have a special area for those items in the corner of the signboard. We call it the "parking lot." Every few weeks, we check on the status of parking lot items, but we don't do this daily.

Problem: Bugs impacting team

Software development is prone to defects, even with strong done rules in place. Usually, dealing with operational issues (tickets) or ordinary bugs is a regular part of doing business, like email or other daily overhead. The effort required is already factored into the average work rates used to determine WIP limits and doesn't need to be tracked on the signboard (assuming you already have online systems for tracking bugs and tickets).

However, sometimes fixing a particular bug or an operational issue is as much work as other product improvements. These tricky issues are managed like any other work item. You create a note card, order it against the rest of the backlog, and slot it into its proper place. These complex issues typically need to be specified, implemented, and verified like any other product work.

> **Note** If all your team does is fix bugs or handle tickets, Kanban can be an excellent way to manage your bug or ticket backlog efficiently. In that case, every note card is a bug or ticket, and the steps are the ones used to resolve those items. For more details, see Chapter 8, "Sustained engineering."

Problem: Item needs design work

Sometimes an item in the backlog is so complex that an analyst needs extra time to specify it and break it down. Often this involves some user experience design, architectural design, and perhaps experimental design. (My favorite approach to design work is called *Scenario-Focused Engineering*, which I describe in more detail in Chapter 9.) The design work is a task unto itself, so you make the design work a separate work item on the signboard.

The Specify step for design work is breaking down the work into smaller tasks. The Implement step for those tasks is creating the design. The Validate step for those tasks is reviewing the design and getting it signed off. When it's done, you've got a completed design, which then adds several new items to the backlog.

Yes, approaching design work as though it were product work is a bit of a stretch. Ideally, you'd use a separate signboard with steps specific to design work. You should do this if a separate team is assigned to design or if you want to use a separate swim lane for design work (more details in Chapter 9). However, using the same signboard for occasional design work does function quite well in practice, and we are Kanban pragmatists. We're trying to deliver value to our customers in the most efficient manner and with the highest quality possible. If that means altering the done rules occasionally to fit design work instead of product work, so be it.

Problem: Important review, demo, or conference approaching

Sometimes, major work has to get done that isn't design work or product work—it's preparing for an executive review, fashioning a demo for customers, authoring a conference presentation, or some other significant task. How do you account for this time on your signboard? The same way you account for design work—add a note card to the backlog. Be flexible. Define special done rules to suit the current work. And then deliver the work on time with high quality. Don't worry; the imaginary Kanban police won't mind.

Problem: New work, plan changes, and updated requirements

New work can arrive at any time, plans can change, and requirements can be updated. When change happens, do the following:

- Write note cards for new items.

- Reorder the backlog to account for changes in priorities or to slot in new items.

- Leave items already in work alone, except to edit them if their requirements have changed.

Even though priorities may have changed, there's usually no reason to abandon work in progress. Newly prioritized work will move into the flow in less than a week. That's because work in progress is limited, so waiting time is short.

In the rare event that new work must commence immediately, you can move active cards to a Track column and free up space for the new items.

> **Note** No special planning meetings are necessary to account for new work, plan changes, or updated requirements.

Problem: Item needs to be assigned to a busy team member

Sometimes work items are uniquely suited to a particular team member because of that person's expertise or past experience. If that team member is busy with another item or otherwise unavailable, you've got a few choices:

- Assign the item to another person and have the preferred team member provide review and oversight. This is a great option for spreading knowledge across your team and backing up the preferred team member. (You never want one person to be a bottleneck.)

- Reassign the preferred team member's current work to another person.

- Move the card to the Track column until the preferred team member is available.

- Lower the order of the item in the backlog.

Problem: Some team members like doing more than one item at a time

When you limit work in progress to one item per team member, plus a 50 percent buffer, people are basically assigned only one work item at a time. Working on one item at a time avoids costly context switches and truly focuses your attention. There's always email or other minor work to do if you're ever stuck.

However, some people work best with clumps of related work. It's not ideal from the perspective of minimizing work in progress, but accommodating different work styles is important to a cohesive team. If your team has such a person, increase the WIP limit for this person's step by one or two (giving him 2–3 items at once). It's not ideal, and should be used only when the person's productivity is clearly negatively impacted by the lower WIP limit.

Problem: Can't find time to improve tools and automation

Customers, partners, and management can be demanding. With these demands, it's hard to find time to improve your own team's tools and automation. However, it's those infrastructure improvements that enable you to deliver more work in less time and at higher quality (just like with Kanban).

The solution is to put tool and automation improvements on note cards, just as you do for product improvements, and order them in your backlog accordingly. One or 2 items in 10 should be infrastructure improvements—after all, there's always room for improvement.

Problem: New person joins the team

When a new person joins the team, WIP limits may need to be adjusted. Ideally, that person is assigned to the slowest step (increasing its throughput). If so, simply work through the process described in "Step 3: Set limits on chaos" again. If the new person is assigned to a different step, she is going to have free time or her peers will. That time can be used wisely by helping with other projects. Remember, you can't go faster than your slowest step.

Problem: Team has long design discussions during standup

Daily standup meetings should take 5–15 minutes. Sometimes teams get into design discussions as they address new items or handle blocking issues. A brief overview is fine, but long discussions should take place at a different time. Some of my teams schedule a conference room for an hour after their daily standup for design discussions. They don't use it every day, but it's there when they need it.

Problem: Some team members can't attend standup

Sometimes team members can't attend the daily standup meeting. Perhaps they are working from home that day or are on a trip. Team members can ask other team members to move note cards for them at any time. They can also send their status to the project manager, attend standup via telecommunications, or use an online meeting.

If you have team members spread across significant distances, you'll need to use a virtual signboard and have online standup meetings.

Problem: Team focusing too much on process details

Some team members may be quite passionate about process. In their effort to be pure, do things "the right way," or simply comply with what they see as "hard rules," team members can focus too much on process details in place of delivering high-quality value to customers. Those team members may think that following rules and practices precisely is necessary to deliver high-quality value to customers.

Following the rules and guidelines in this book is important to a team just starting with Kanban. However, over time your team will internalize visualizing its work and limiting work in progress. Team members will naturally swarm to blocked steps and avoid working on too much at once. At that point, being flexible is an important part of being efficient.

You don't want to compromise on quality, but you should trust your team to operate in the manner that best suits its makeup and current needs. If you find that quality or efficiency has dropped significantly, you can always return to a stricter approach.

Checklist

Here's a checklist of actions to quickly start using Kanban:

- ❏ Capture your team's high-level routine as a series of steps.

  - If you are unsure, start with the steps Specify, Implement, and Validate.

- ❏ Redecorate your wall with a Kanban board that has a Backlog column and two columns for each of your steps.

- ❏ Set limits on chaos that restrict the maximum number of work items (cards) for each step. These are known as work-in-progress (WIP) limits.

- ❏ Define done rules for each step that must be met before a work item (card) can be moved from the Active to the Done column for that step.

- ❏ Run your daily standup at a set time each day, focusing on issues that block work from progressing (cards from moving between columns).

- ❏ As needed, update your organization's tracking system with your team's current status.

- ❏ As needed, adjust your WIP limits and done rules to ensure quality work that flows smoothly through your signboard.

- ❏ As needed, add a Track column between the Active and Done columns of your implementation step to track external input that is blocking implementation of a work item (such as a late or an unstable dependency).

- ❏ As needed, add new items (cards) and reorder items in your backlog.

CHAPTER 3

Hitting deadlines

Kanban's simple approach to delivering value to your customers efficiently and with high quality also provides the predictable scheduling and staffing data you need to deliver that value on time and on budget.

Kanban provides predictability through constraining work in progress (WIP)—the same technique it uses to control chaos. As I describe in Chapter 2, "Kanban quick-start guide," thoughtfully limiting WIP allows your team to respond quickly to changes and prevents issues from festering, all while making your delivery of value to customers smooth, continuous, and efficient.

Limiting WIP also constrains your team's size (your costs) and reduces your cycle time (the time for a planned work item to go from specification through validation). Shortening cycle time benefits quality, agility, and customer engagement. It also allows you to accurately measure throughput, and thus accurately estimate completion dates.

The following sections will help you plan your project and staff your team:

Populate your backlog
Establish your minimum viable product (MVP)
Order work, including technical debt
Estimate features and tasks
Track expected completion date
Right-size your team
Checklist

Populate your backlog

Populating your work backlog is trivial if your feature team (3–10 people) is part of a larger effort and your work backlog is determined by your internal partners or customers (including bugs and tickets if you run an operational team). In that case, simply write a descriptive name for each of the features, improvements, and work items you need to accomplish on its own note card, and then place those note cards in the Backlog column of your signboard. (You'll prioritize them into buckets in a later step.) You're done.

If your team gets to determine your own backlog of work, you have some product planning to do. Product improvements (demands on your team) come from two sources:

- **Your customers** Between usage patterns you can learn about through instrumentation, experiments you can run online, feedback you can receive through forums, and issues you can track from customer support, you've likely got a long list of potential product improvements. Write a descriptive name for each improvement on its own note card, and then place the cards in the Backlog column. To help you order and recognize cards later, you can put a U, X, F, or S in a card's corner to indicate its origin: usage, experiment, feedback, and support, respectively.

- **Your business** Your leadership likely has ideas about how they want to improve the business, even if you work for a nonprofit. Your team, and your internal and external partners, likely have ideas about great new features and technology they want to add and bugs they want to fix. Write a descriptive name for each idea on its own note card, and then place the cards in the Backlog column. To help you order and recognize cards later, you can put an L, TF, PF, or B in a card's corner to indicate its origin: leadership, team feature, partner feature, and bug, respectively.

By now, you should have far too many cards in your backlog. The next couple of steps will help you sort them.

Inside Xbox

Some of my Xbox teams were part of larger efforts, and their high-level feature backlogs were basically determined by product-wide planning. However, my teams would add design details, bugs, infrastructure improvements, and specific support issues to their backlogs.

The ordering of features was determined in concert with our peer teams at a quarterly planning day.

- We taped every team's pending high-level features on the wall, blocked by months.

- Then teams would "walk the wall" to check for timing issues with dependencies or question how much really fits in each month (considering vacations, events, and other concerns).

- Next was "speed dating." Each team could sign up to meet with any other team for 15 minutes to discuss conflicts and ordering. We'd typically go through three to five rounds of speed dating before all conflicts were resolved.

- Then it was time for one last chance to walk the updated wall, before the combined teams agreed to the plan (if no one objected).

With a plan in place, the features were transferred in order onto team backlogs. The high-level features were broken down into tasks as they completed the Specify step, and work became production-ready quickly.

Some of my Xbox teams have worked as isolated service teams. We built their backlogs from customer and partner requests, leadership requests, and improvement ideas from the team. Not as much coordination with other teams was required.

I provide more detail about experiences like these in Chapter 7, "Using Kanban within large organizations."

Establish your minimum viable product (MVP)

You can skip this section if you run a continuously deployed service or an operational team and all you need to do is order incoming work. Otherwise, you are probably involved in a product release (first release or an update) and need to determine your minimum viable product (MVP).

For the purposes of ordering your backlog, your MVP is the set of work items (note cards) in your backlog that *must* be completed before release. That is, regardless of the monetary or market impact, you would delay or cancel your product release if those work items were incomplete. (Detailed information about establishing your MVP can be found online and from a variety of sources.)

If you are being honest with yourself and your leadership, the number of work items making up the MVP is a very small percentage of the total backlog. There are items you really should have, items you'd like to have, and items you don't care as much about. None of those items are in the MVP. The only items in the MVP are items you really must have. Typically, MVP items are basic functionality that customers expect before they'd even try your product, plus just enough differentiation to determine whether your new release is desirable.

> **Tip**   Defining a true MVP that you prioritize above all else is an excellent way to hit your deadlines and avoid unused specifications, incomplete and untested features, and unused tests. You'll hit your deadlines because the MVP is usually a small percentage of your backlog, yet once the MVP is done, you'll have a product you can release. You'll avoid unfinished work because all the work you do on MVP items is essential and won't be abandoned. (In contrast, one of the best ways to cause a product to slip is to leave critical work until the very end.)

A simple, fast, and effective means of determining your MVP is running a bucketing and affinity exercise with your team, its leadership, and some representative customers and partners. You gather in a room and sort through the cards in your backlog. The sorting can be done on a large whiteboard, a corkboard, or the top of a large table, which is divided into four buckets. Together you sort all your items into the following buckets:

- **Must have**   MVP, sometimes called "pri 0"

- **Should have**   Priority 1

- **Like to have**   Priority 2

- **Nice ideas**   Priority 3

While sorting, you'll notice that the cards often clump together into related work (clusters). It's useful to keep clusters together (with tape, pins, paper clips, or otherwise), and perhaps even name the cluster with a new high-level card. Related work items can sometimes fall into different buckets.

Naturally, people will disagree about bucket assignments. With everyone in the room, you can discuss controversial items, come to a shared understanding of the work and its importance, and then place it with confidence. The more critical an item's priority, the more scrutiny you should give it. In particular, you should always question MVP items: "Would we really hold up the release for that?"

When your sorting meeting is finished (typically in two to four hours), you'll have a clear definition of your next release. It will have all the MVP items, many of the pri 1 items, and some of the easy pri 2 and 3 items that are closely aligned with higher-priority items. The next step seeds the first set of these items into the backlog in order.

Order work, including technical debt

At this point, you've got your backlog of work items sorted into large prioritized buckets. (Operational teams typically assign prioritized buckets to bugs and tickets each day or upon creation based on well-defined rules.) These work items should be a mix of improvements garnered from customer usage, experiments, feedback, and customer support; feature and technology requests from business leadership, team members, and partners; and a variety of technical debt.

> **Note** Technical debt refers to unresolved bugs, legacy code in need of refactoring, tools that need to be upgraded, and components that require redesign. Basically, technical debt is quality-improvement work that you've postponed. It's referred to as debt because the longer you let it fester, the more expensive it becomes to resolve (much like financial debt).

Ordering these cards in your backlog is a team activity. Leadership, internal and external partners, and customers help you prioritize the cards into the big buckets, but day-to-day execution belongs to the team.

Once your team is practiced at ordering, team members can do it themselves at any time, as needed, based on the prioritized buckets. To gain initial experience, gather your team around your signboard and work together to order your backlog, based on the following rules:

- You don't want to overwhelm your signboard and its backlog space, so place your cards in four piles next to your signboard.

- Team members then place all pri 0 bucket items (the MVP) in the backlog area.

- Related items within the same bucket should stay together, ordered by their natural sequence of execution.

- Items that can be started immediately (no dependencies) should be ordered first, followed by items that can be done soon afterward, and so on.

- After you place all your pri 0 items, if your backlog area still has room, begin placing the pri 1 items using the same approach.

- Take any pri 0 or lower items that don't fit in the backlog, and leave them in piles next to your signboard. You can use those piles, in order, to occasionally refill the backlog.

Notice that only a relatively small number of cards are actually put in order—after all, the backlog area on your signboard isn't that big. That's intentional: the order of work can be quite fluid because markets, customer and partner requirements, and leadership direction frequently change. You strictly order only enough work to get started. The rest of the cards remain in their prioritized buckets.

> **Tip** After you order the cards, it's possible that no pri 0 items can begin work immediately because of incomplete dependencies. If that happens, those items will naturally move to the Track column under Implement, and pri 1 items will receive attention until pri 0 items are unblocked. Even better, your team can pull work items from your dependencies, move them onto your signboard, and help unblock your dependencies yourselves. For more on the Track column, including a diagram, check "Item blocked awaiting external input" in the "Troubleshooting" section of Chapter 2.

With a populated backlog, your team can manage its work as described in the Kanban quick-start guide (Chapter 2). Only continue on to the next sections if your leadership and partners want to know when you'll be finished, or if you need to right-size your team to hit a specific deadline.

Estimate features and tasks

Prediction of future events that don't neatly fit the laws of physics is a precarious endeavor. However, your leadership, customers, and internal and external partners may need to know when to expect certain results. In particular:

- **How soon will a work item be addressed and done?** This is a common requirement of internal and external partners who depend on your team and must schedule around it.

- **When will a significant product release be completed?** This is a common requirement of leadership, product planners, and marketers who need to set proper expectations in the market around timing and your feature set.

> **Tip** If your leadership, customers, or partners aren't asking these kinds of questions, there's no need to estimate features and tasks or track the expected completion date—you can skip the remaining sections. If they are asking these questions, estimation is a necessary exercise.

Work items come in all different sizes, so it's hard to predict how long any particular item will take, let alone a whole backlog of items. However, the Specify step from the Kanban quick-start guide

(Chapter 2) breaks down differently sized items into smaller, similarly sized items (typically taking one to five days each to complete). For clarity, I'll refer to these smaller items as *tasks*.

The time needed to complete tasks is more predictable than for the larger and more varied original work items. Thus, your estimation job involves the following steps:

- **Estimate the number of tasks needed to complete work items**   I recommend using a Wideband Delphi method, which utilizes iteration and consensus to provide accurate estimates. My favorite method is a simplified form of Wideband Delphi called "planning poker." To estimate task breakdown using planning poker, team members sit around a table (or an online messaging room), and each team member privately estimates the number of tasks needed to complete the work item in question. They can write their estimates on a slip of paper or use preprinted cards. (Planning poker cards typically follow a geometric or Fibonacci sequence.) Everyone reveals his or her estimate simultaneously so that no one exerts undue influence. If the estimates match, you're done (write the estimate on the work item note card). If they differ, the high and low estimators explain themselves, the team members discuss their thinking, and then the process repeats until the estimates agree. The process also identifies assumptions before they become problems.

- **Calculate your task completion rate**   To do this, count the number of tasks that are done with their final step within any two-week to four-week period, and divide by the number of days. (For teams that average around three days per task, like mine, a sample of two to four weeks should be sufficient.) Note that the task completion rate isn't the reciprocal of the average time required to complete a task (the task's cycle time). That's because the task completion rate accounts for all team members and all steps (including the Specify step, which breaks down items of variable size into tasks of similar size).

- **Let your leadership, customers, and internal and external partners know when to expect results**   Use the appropriate formula from the following table (active tasks are those that are in work but haven't finished the last step, which includes tasks in the Track column):

Question	Estimate (in days)
How soon will a work item be addressed and done?	(active tasks + estimated tasks for the work item and the work items ahead of it) / task completion rate
When will a significant product release be completed?	(active tasks + estimated tasks for MVP work items) / task completion rate

Please note:

- The product release estimate is for completing the minimum viable product (MVP), not any pri 1 or 2 items. That's because after the MVP is complete, you should by definition be able to release the product. Be sure to emphasize this fact to interested leadership, customers, and partners, reiterating which features encompass the MVP. They may want to add more items and have you update your estimate.

- It's helpful for team members to compare the estimated number of tasks for a work item (written on the note card) with the actual number of tasks after that work item is specified. Over time, the team should get better at estimation.

- The steps I've listed to estimate features and tasks are fast, easy, and fairly accurate. Spending more time on estimation doesn't lead to greater accuracy, but it does take time away from delivering value to customers.

- The estimating formula used (pending tasks divided by the task completion rate) calculates what's often referred to as "lead time." This concept is derived from Little's Law, which states that the work in progress in a system (pending tasks) is equal to the average system throughput (task completion rate) multiplied by the system response time (lead time). You can read more about Little's Law in Chapter 9, "Further resources and beyond."

- None of these estimates account for significant delays that result from dependencies or changes in plans. That's covered in the next section of this chapter.

Inside Xbox

When my teams first switched from Scrum to Kanban, we estimated by using "story points." Story points are a team-specific measure of size. The team estimates how many story points each work item encompasses (using planning poker) and then tracks how many story points can be completed within a certain time interval (often a Scrum sprint of one to four weeks).

After a month or two of using Kanban, it became clear that broken-down tasks were roughly the same size and took roughly the same amount of time (the same number of story points). Thus, estimating tasks achieves the same goal as estimating story points, but tasks seem more concrete to leadership (and some team members).

My current teams rarely do estimation. Estimates were needed at first because our customers and partners demanded them. After several months, our track record of delivering value continuously and consistently built trust with our customers and partners. They knew we'd deliver reliably and sought estimates only on rare occasions. Naturally, we still supply estimates when asked by following the approach described in this chapter.

Track expected completion date

Early estimates can't account for significant delays that result from dependencies and changes in plans. In addition, task completion rates change and task estimates improve. If your leadership, customers, or partners want to be updated regularly on when to expect work items or when the product release will be completed, you need to regularly adjust your estimates to the changing conditions.

There are three values to track (two mentioned in the previous section, and one new value):

- **Task completion rate (TCR)**   You can track TCR as a moving average or monthly updated value (tasks completed per day). Doing so helps account for delays and changing team dynamics.

- **Current task estimate (CTE)**   This is the total number of active tasks and estimated pending tasks (including tasks in a Track column). The CTE is essential for updated estimates because it represents remaining work.

- **Task add rate (TAR)**   This value wasn't used in the previous section because it measures changes in plans, not initial estimates. You subtract the total number of tasks (pending, active, and done) at the start of a month from the total number at the end and divide by the number of days. This gives you the tasks added per day (or tasks cut if the value is negative) and accounts for plan changes and feature bloat.

These three values are readily available in Kanban (you just count the cards and estimates on the signboard). A few notes:

- My teams count weekend days because folks sometimes do work on weekends, but you can count just weekdays as long as you're consistent for both task completion rate and task add rate.

- I choose a month as the regular interval, but you can use fewer or more days so long as you're consistent.

- The pending tasks in the current task estimate are typically the count of pending MVP tasks, but they could be any set of tasks of interest to your leadership, customers, or partners.

With values for task completion rate, current task estimate, and task add rate in hand, you can calculate the number of days until your team will complete the current task set. It's CTE / (TCR − TAR). To understand why, I've included an example of a Cumulative Flow Diagram (Figure 3-1), which is a stacked column chart showing the number of pending, active, and done tasks over time.

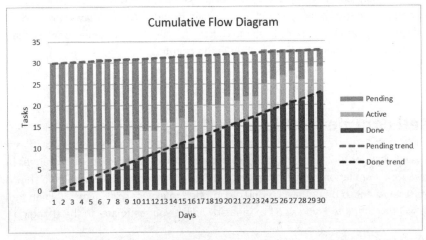

FIGURE 3-1 Cumulative Flow Diagram showing the accumulation of pending, active, and done tasks over time.

The current task estimate is the combined top and middle height (pending and active tasks). The task add rate is the slope of the line at the top. The task completion rate is the slope of the line in the middle. The current set of tasks will be complete where the lines meet. The values from the Cumulative Flow Diagram are shown in the following worksheet. (You can download an Excel spreadsheet with the formulas. See the book's introduction for details.)

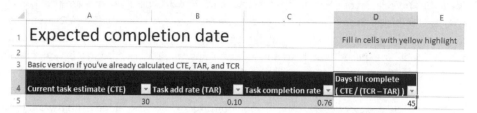

The calculation shows that the initial 30 tasks will be completed 45 days from the start of the project (a little more than two weeks after the last day on the chart). You can estimate the number of days remaining from any point by replacing 30 with the number of pending and active tasks from any day. The actual completion date will be roughly the same, given that the task add rate and task completion rate haven't changed significantly.

> **Tip** If your task add rate (TAR) is larger than your task completion rate (TCR), you'll never finish. For projects of somewhat fixed scope that are under intense scrutiny, it serves you well to regularly track current task estimate, task add rate, and task completion rate, as well as your expected completion date. They form a compelling argument to keep the scope of your project under control.

Right-size your team

Once you calculate the expected completion date of your project, your leadership, customers, or partners may have concerns.

- Perhaps you run a continuously deployed service or an operational team and release dates aren't significant—you release continuously. However, leadership wants to size your team to fit the flow of incoming requests. How many people should you keep on staff?

- Perhaps the date is sooner than required. Leadership could simply ask the team to complete as many pri 1 and pri 2 items as possible in the time allotted. However, leadership may decide to reassign some team members to other needy projects. How many people should you keep to complete the project on time?

- Here's the big concern: perhaps the expected completion date is later than required. Leadership could ask your team to work weekends, but that's not sustainable and can lead to poor design and poor quality from a weary team with little time to think. Leadership could cut more from the minimum viable product (in which case it really wasn't the minimum). However, leadership often considers putting more resources on the project. How many people do you need to complete the project on time?

Before I show some calculations for right-sizing your team, there are a couple of important considerations:

- The following calculations assume that team capacity grows linearly with team size. However, as Frederick P. Brooks Jr. pointed out in *The Mythical Man-Month* (1995), cross-team communication grows geometrically with team size. Thus, you can't double team size and expect double the throughput. Kanban's focus on smooth flow, visualizing work, and minimal meetings significantly reduces the impact of cross-team communication, but you still need to account for big team changes. Should the following calculations dictate that your team double or triple in size, consider refactoring your project into several teams that work together through a shared architecture and established interfaces.

- Adding new people to a team always slows it down before it speeds it up. New team members take a while to learn what they need to be productive, and veteran team members spend time answering questions and helping new team members acclimate. As a result, the time to add people is at the beginning or in the midst of the project—never at the end. (At the end of a project, you're better off slipping the release date or reducing the functionality.)

You can calculate the required size of your feature team in two ways:

- Use a basic approach before your team has measured its current task estimate (CTE), task add rate (TAR), and task completion rate (TCR). The basic approach requires only the same basic data that's used to determine your initial WIP limits in the Kanban quick-start guide (Chapter 2).

- Use an advanced approach after your team has detailed data about the current task estimate (CTE), task add rate (TAR), and task completion rate (TCR), as described earlier in the section "Track expected completion date."

Basic approach

Let's start with the basic approach. Say, you're putting together a team that has four months to release 25 new feature improvements to your product. (All the formulas and tables that follow are available in an Excel spreadsheet that you can download.)

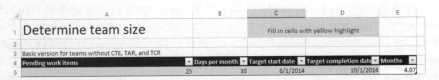

	A	B	C	D	E
1	Determine team size		Fill in cells with yellow highlight		
2					
3	Basic version for teams without CTE, TAR, and TCR				
4	Pending work items	Days per month	Target start date	Target completion date	Months
5	25	30	6/1/2014	10/1/2014	4.07

Note that the months are normalized to 30 days each, thus the count of 4.07 months. If you run a continuously deployed service or an operational team and just want to size your team to fit the flow of incoming requests, enter the number of requests per month as the count of pending work items, and use the start and end dates of a typical month.

Next, let's say you've got the same kind of team I used as an example in the Kanban quick-start guide (Chapter 2). Here's a worksheet showing the team-size calculation.

7	Step	Specify	Implement	Validate
8	A: Average rate per month per person	6	2	3
9	B: Slowest rate (minimum A column)		2	
10	C: Estimated people required for step B (Items / Months / B)		3.07	
11	D: Throughput of step B (B * C)		6.15	
12	E: People needed to match B's throughput (D / A)	1.02	3.07	2.05
13	F: WIP limits (E * 1½ rounded up)	2	5	4

For the example:

- **A**   On average, each analyst can specify roughly six items per month, each developer can implement roughly two items a month, and each tester can validate roughly three items per month. (You can use a shorter time frame by changing the number of days per month.)

- **B**   Implementing is the slowest step (two items per month per person).

- **C**   We want to estimate the number of developers required to implement 25 work items in 4.07 months. Since the developers can implement two items per month, you need 25 / 4.07 / 2 = 3.07 developers.

- **D**   The throughput is 2 * 3.07 = 6.15 items per month (the extra hundredth is the result of Excel storing all these data values with higher precision).

- **E**   Dividing that throughput by the average rates for each step gives you the people needed for each step (1.02 analysts, 3.07 developers, and 2.05 testers).

- **F**   You calculate the WIP limits as in the Kanban quick-start guide (Chapter 2) by adding a 50 percent buffer to the people totals and rounding up (2 for Specify, 5 for Implement, and 4 for Validate).

As in the Kanban quick-start guide, the WIP limits from the worksheet are starting values. The limits should be adjusted to maximize team output and agility. Check the Kanban quick-start guide's "Troubleshooting" section for when and how to adjust WIP limits for the best outcomes.

The people counts are also approximate starting values, which is why I left them as decimals. Once you form your team and start work, you can track your expected completion date over time and fine-tune the team as needed.

Advanced approach

The basic approach uses average work item rates per person per step to calculate the necessary team size. As I discussed in the estimation portions of this chapter, work item size has a great deal of variability. You get better estimates by breaking down work items into tasks and measuring actual task completion rates.

If you have the current task estimate (CTE), task add rate (TAR), and task completion rate (TCR), as described in the "Track expected completion date" section, you can estimate the proper team size with a bit more confidence.

			Days till complete			Estimated /	
17 Advanced version for teams with established CTE, TAR, and TCR							
18 Current task estimate (CTE)	Task add rate (TAR)	Task completion rate (TCR)	(CTE / (TCR − TAR))	Target start date	Target completion date	Days	Expected
19	100	0.10	0.76	152	6/1/2014	10/1/2014	122	1.24

For a comparison with the basic approach, I set the current task estimate to 100 (four tasks per basic-example work item), used the task add rate and task completion rate from the previous section, and the same 4.07 month period as for the basic example (122 days). I use days instead of months because task add rate and task completion rate are measured in days.

The estimated number of days needed to complete 100 tasks is 152, but the number of days available is 122. The ratio between the estimated and expected number of days is 152 / 122 = 1.24—that's the multiple of team members we need.

21 Step	Specify	Implement	Validate
22 A: Current WIP limits	2	5	3
23 B: Current people engaged (A ÷ 1½ rounded down)	1	3	2
24 C: Estimated people required (B * Estim / Expect)	1.24	3.73	2.48
25 D: Estimated WIP limits (C * 1½ rounded up)	2	6	4

In this example:

- **A**   Rather than relying on the number of current team members assigned, who may not be fully dedicated to the team with the 0.76 task completion rate, we use the WIP limits that control flow.

- **B**   We divide the limits by 1.5 and round down to determine the number of people completing 0.76 tasks a day. (That's the inverse of our algorithm to get the WIP limits.)

- **C**   We then multiply by 1.24, the ratio between the estimated and expected number of days. This results in estimates for the number of people needed to complete the 100 tasks in 122 days.

- **D**   Adding 50 percent to those people totals and rounding up gives you each step's WIP limit (2 for Specify, 6 for Implement, and 4 for Validate).

Note that the WIP limits and people estimates differ between the advanced approach and the basic approach. Two reasons account for this:

- If you assume four tasks per work item, the throughput for the basic-approach example would be 6.15 * 4 = 24.6 tasks per month, for a task completion rate of 24.6 / 30 days = 0.82 tasks per day. That's slightly higher than 0.76 tasks per day we used in the advanced approach example.

- The basic approach doesn't account for the task add rate (0.1 tasks per day). Over 122 days, that's 12.2 additional tasks to complete.

As with the basic approach, WIP limits and people counts derived through the advanced approach are just starting values. You should adjust them as your team does the real work and gets real feedback data.

Because Kanban continuously provides you with updated data on your project, it's easy to adjust your estimates, WIP limits, and team sizes to hit your deadlines. In time, your delivery of customer value becomes so predictable that estimation is easy and scheduling accuracy is less of a concern.

Checklist

Here's a checklist of actions to ensure that you hit your deadlines:

- ❏ Collect product-improvement ideas from your customers and your business, putting descriptive names for each idea on its own card.

    - Include an indicator on each card for the source of the idea (helps with ordering and recognition of the cards).

- ❏ Place the cards into one of four buckets: must-have and wouldn't release without (pri 0: the minimum viable product), should have (pri 1), like to have (pri 2) and nice ideas (pri 3).

- ❏ Order a subset of the cards in the Backlog column of your signboard, selecting first from the minimum viable product and then augmenting with related or additional lower-priority cards as needed.

- ❏ As needed, let your leadership, customers, and internal and external partners know when to expect results.

    - Estimate the number of tasks needed to complete work items, preferably using a Wideband Delphi method such as planning poker.

    - Calculate your task completion rate (divide the number of tasks that are done with their final steps within any two-week to four-week period by the number of days in that period).

    - Report the estimated date by dividing the total estimated number of tasks in consideration by the task completion rate, and adding that number of days to the current date.

- ❏ As needed, track and report your expected completion date for your leadership, customers, or partners.

    - Compute your task completion rate (TCR), current task estimate (CTE), and task add rate (TAR).

    - Calculate your expected completion date by adding the result of CTE / (TCR − TAR) to the current date.

- ❏ As needed, right-size your team to complete your project on time, using one of two methods.

    - Use a basic approach to calculate the number of people needed for each step, based on average rates per month per person for each step.

    - Use an advanced approach to calculate the number of people needed for each step, based on task completion rate (TCR), current task estimate (CTE), and task add rate (TAR).

CHAPTER 4

Adapting from Waterfall

This chapter is for people currently using a traditional Waterfall method for product development. If your team uses Scrum, please feel free to skip to the next chapter, "Evolving from Scrum."

Kanban is simple in structure and uses common terminology. As a result, a wide range of people can begin using it without significant trouble or prolonged explanation. As with any new method, it takes a few weeks to adjust to Kanban and a few months to master it. Nonetheless, even if you learned product development decades ago, you can quickly get started and feel productive with Kanban. After a couple of months, the increases in productivity, quality, predictability, and agility should be evident and measurable to your leadership and your team.

When I talk about "traditional Waterfall," I mean the practice of writing specs, implementing features, and performing validation in bulk (many features at once) over the course of milestones that often span months. I've experienced many variations of Waterfall at Microsoft, Boeing, and other places where I've worked.

This chapter will help you adapt your variation of traditional Waterfall to Kanban without much fuss or hassle. I've even included a rude Q & A listing questions that a blunt team member might ask, followed by pragmatic answers meant to reassure, build trust in the new approach, and clearly explain how to achieve great results with Kanban.

The topics covered are:

Introducing Kanban to a Waterfall team
Working in feature teams
Completing features before starting new ones
Dealing with specs and bugs
Engaging with customers
Celebrating performance improvements
Rude Q & A
Checklist

Introducing Kanban to a Waterfall team

A traditional Waterfall team is one that likely has members who've been doing product development for decades. Their habits were formed long ago and have served them well over the years. Although the products they build might be buggy initially, the members of the traditional Waterfall team know how to stabilize the product at the end, drive out the bugs, and release reasonably close to the scheduled date with acceptable quality.

However, as product development has moved to shorter timelines, and long stabilization periods are no longer viable, traditional Waterfall teams may be pressured to become "agile." This can make team members feel both uncomfortable with the notion of change and disrespected given their past accomplishments.

For a traditional Waterfall team to embrace Kanban, you need to explain why a change is necessary, utilize people's valuable Waterfall experience, and lightly adjust their familiar methods to facilitate a smooth workflow and quick cadence. Once the team masters Kanban, it can choose to improve further by making more significant adjustments to its approach. However, the starting point can feel familiar and straightforward.

To understand why making some adjustments to Waterfall is necessary, it's helpful to recognize where a traditional Waterfall approach breaks down:

- When traditional Waterfall is done well, you start with a solid plan everyone believes in (based on market research, prototyping, architectural design, and other planning), with clearly documented requirements and specifications and a thoughtful schedule based on known dependencies and staff allocations. Such plans typically prescribe a year or more of product development, broken into a series of milestones followed by a prolonged stabilization period.

- Unfortunately, within a few months of implementing the plan, uncertainties creep in, requirements change, dependencies shift, and people move around. As a result, the team has to update plans, specifications, and schedules and throw out or rework the portions of the product (and associated tests, if any) that are affected.

- The cycle of updates, discarded work, and rework repeats as the market shifts during product development and customers provide feedback at each milestone.

- All the plan and product churn results in numerous quality issues that often extend the already long stabilization period, frequently delaying the product release.

Ideally, every product change should receive immediate customer feedback, adjusting to market shifts daily, with no buildup of churn or other quality issues. Doing so would require a smooth flow of work through each development step and a continuous development approach that delivers completed, high-quality product improvements every day.

> **Tip** Even secret products and new breakthrough products have customers and benefit from frequent customer feedback. You might need to be selective in choosing the customers you use, but their feedback is essential for delivering a high-quality, delightful product.

Scrum tries to address the breakdowns in traditional Waterfall by converting the milestones to short sprints (typically one to four weeks in length), producing customer-ready product improvements each sprint, and adjusting to customer feedback at the end of each sprint. It's a substantial improvement, but churn still builds up during sprints, plans still need to be updated each sprint, and the flow of customer-ready product enhancements, with its immediate customer feedback, is more frequent but still not smooth or continuous.

Kanban is built for smooth and continuous delivery of customer value. It carefully controls the flow and quality of work to discover and resolve issues immediately. It limits the work in progress (what's called *inventory* in manufacturing) so that churn doesn't build up and the team and product can adjust to market shifts daily. Kanban does all this while working within the current roles and specialties of traditional Waterfall teams, making it seem familiar and straightforward.

When introducing Kanban to a Waterfall team, start by reassuring team members. Tell them, "Nearly everything you did before to develop products, you still get to do. You don't have to learn new roles or unfamiliar terminology. We will put a big focus on quality, and we will do our best to frontload the most critical work. But you will still do day-to-day product development the way you always have. The biggest change will be the way you select what to do next. Luckily, that selection process is easy and displayed on a big board where everyone can see it."

At this point, you can proceed to the Kanban quick-start guide (Chapter 2) using your current backlog of work as a starting point. But before you move on, here are a few points about the rest of this chapter.

- A couple of areas that might take traditional Waterfall team members by surprise are worth discussing in advance. I cover these in the next two sections: "Working in feature teams" and "Completing features before starting new ones."

- After your feature team has gotten used to Kanban, you might choose to change how you deal with specs and bugs and how you engage with customers. I describe those changes in the sections "Dealing with specs and bugs" and "Engaging with customers."

- To show your management and your team how Kanban is improving productivity and quality, you'll want to measure and celebrate your progress. This can be critical to gain commitment to Kanban, it's easy, and it provides a nice morale boost. See the "Celebrating performance improvements" section.

- Finally, I have answers to common questions in the last section, "Rude Q & A."

Inside Xbox

I've moved three traditional Waterfall teams to Kanban: two software development teams and one operations team. A few people on the teams were familiar with Scrum and agile techniques, and some had worked with virtual feature teams, but most had only used traditional Waterfall.

Complaints were rare during adoption. Team members found Kanban straightforward and the signboard quite helpful. Most of the confusion and questions were about the WIP limits and dealing with occasional work items that didn't match typical work.

I observed the first few standup meetings with each team and answered any questions that arose. Each team used the Specify, Implement, and Validate steps I describe in the Kanban quick-start guide. Those steps are familiar to traditional Waterfall teams. (Some of my teams called the Specify step "Breakdown" but still used it for specification.)

After the first few standup meetings, I attended only occasionally. When questions came up about WIP limits or unusual work items, team members would stop by my office and ask, "What are we supposed to do?" I captured those questions, and the answers, in the troubleshooting section of the Kanban quick-start guide in Chapter 2.

Working in feature teams

Kanban brings feature teams together each day to view the signboard and handle blocking issues. A feature team is a group of individuals, often from multiple disciplines, who work on the same set of product features together.

A typical feature team might have 1–3 analysts, 1–6 developers, and 1–6 testers (a total of 3–15 people), but some can be larger. Feature teams may also have marketers, product planners, designers, user researchers, architects, technical researchers, data scientists, quality assurance personnel, service engineers, service operations staff, and project managers. Often, feature team members are part of multiple feature teams, although developers and testers tend to be dedicated to a single team.

Many people who use traditional Waterfall work on feature teams, all for the same manager or as a virtual team. However, some groups completely separate different disciplines, using formal handoff procedures between disciplines, including associated documentation.

With Kanban, you can maintain separate disciplines and formal handoff procedures if you prefer. The handoff procedures map directly to the done rules for each step. However, Kanban does require each discipline working on the same workflow to share the same signboard and attend standup together. While this is certainly a change, it's a relatively minor logistical one that is easily incorporated into people's workday.

The key is to pick a time for the standup when all feature team members can attend. My teams schedule theirs at 10:30 a.m. It's late enough in the morning that even folks who sleep in arrive on time, and it's early enough that no one is away at lunch or at an afternoon obligation. Since standup takes only 5–15 minutes, even with large teams, it's over before 10:45 a.m. For teams with remote members, pick the best time you can and use online meeting tools.

While the focus of the standup meeting is to look over the signboard and handle blocking issues, getting everyone together also opens opportunities for cross-discipline team members to connect. Keep the standup focused properly, but after the standup, people can meet and sync up on a variety of scheduling, process, and design issues, while folks not involved in these issues return to their work. It's invaluable to have this regular time when everyone working on the same features can align themselves.

To help everyone adjust to the daily standups, tell your team, "We all work together to create great features for our customers. When we work together, it's helpful to get together daily, see our work progress, and handle any issues that might keep our high-quality work from reaching our customers quickly."

Completing features before starting new ones

Some traditional Waterfall teams specify (and review) every feature in a release before any features are implemented, and some implement every feature before any are validated. Some Waterfall teams arrange release work into a series of Specify/Implement/Validate milestones. Within each milestone, all features for that milestone are specified before they are implemented and implemented before they are validated. This traditional Waterfall approach is reminiscent of batch processing jobs with mainframe computers.

The batch approach in traditional Waterfall is simple and keeps team members focused. However, it can be inefficient and inflexible if the batches are large and can't be easily changed or reordered. Arguably, the biggest change for traditional Waterfall folks adapting to Kanban is to work on very small batches of items, constrained by WIP limits. The active cards in a step form the current batch. Instead of milestones or releases lasting months or even years, the batches last only days at a time. (I talk about coordinating Kanban work within much larger projects in Chapter 7, "Using Kanban within large organizations.")

Although the small batches in Kanban are a new concept, traditional Waterfall folks adapt quickly because the steps they follow to process each batch are the same as they were in traditional Waterfall. They just process only a few items at a time. Typically, two areas of confusion or surprise come with the shift to small batches:

- There's initial confusion about what to do when the WIP limits restrict the flow of batches. I cover those cases in the troubleshooting section of the Kanban quick-start guide (Chapter 2).

- There's confusion or surprise about the increased frequency of cross-discipline interaction. Because Kanban uses very small batches, people responsible for different steps engage with one another more often. At first, this can seem like a distraction. Personal expectations of quiet time, appropriate engagement, and other professional courtesies develop quickly. In time, team members view the increased interaction as a significant improvement because it catches design and implementation flaws early, before they permeate the entire release and become more expensive to repair.

To smooth the adaptation to small batches, tell your team, "We're all familiar with specifying features, implementing them, and validating that they work well for customers. We used to specify, implement, and validate a whole bunch of features at once. It was easy to organize around large batches, but the world changes quickly, and turning big boats takes time. We're now adopting small batches, moving a card on our signboard as each feature, each bit of customer value, gets specified, implemented, and validated. The cards make tracking these small batches easy, and the small batches make it easier to keep pace with the world and the needs of our customers."

Once your feature team is used to meeting together for the daily standup, and the team has become familiar with the dynamics and extra interaction of working on small batches, you might want to introduce and make a couple of more adjustments to further improve your smooth and continuous delivery of customer value. You might want to change how you deal with specs and bugs and how you engage with customers. I describe those changes in the next two sections.

Dealing with specs and bugs

When you complete features before you start new ones, you significantly shorten the time between writing specs and implementing them and between creating bugs and fixing them. In practice, that reduced time leads to the simplified handling of specs and bugs in Kanban.

Specs

Many traditional Waterfall teams write detailed design specification documents ("specs") for every feature, all of which are reviewed and approved before implementation starts. Detailed specs are important because in traditional Waterfall a feature may not be implemented until months after specification, and not be validated until months after implementation. If you don't clearly document the feature in detail, developers won't remember what to implement and testers won't remember what to validate.

Because Kanban uses small batches, the time between specification, implementation, and validation is measured in days instead of months. At first, traditional Waterfall teams might choose to continue writing detailed specs for every feature. However, teams may find that level of formality to be unnecessary because the design is still fresh in everyone's minds.

It's still important to document, review, and approve designs. However, it's often not necessary to transcribe a design and a list of considerations drawn on a whiteboard into a formal document, with detailed explanations of every point so that people remember them months later. Instead, teams often use electronic notebooks, wikis, or other quick authoring tools to capture photos of whiteboards and key points of design discussions. (My teams love OneNote for this purpose.) Those informal documents capture enough of the design for everyone to remember the main attributes, issues, and agreements. Then, as the feature is implemented, details of the design emerge and can be discussed in real time instead of being speculated upon months in advance.

As I point out in the "Troubleshooting" section of the Kanban quick-start guide (Chapter 2), some feature areas or individual features are still so complex that a detailed design document is necessary. Choosing to write a detailed spec should not be a matter of dogma or habit. It should be a decision based on the needs of the team (and the customer, should the customer require it). If a feature or feature area is unclear, or the tradeoffs and architecture are in question, you should write a detailed spec and flesh out the design. Otherwise, a quick, informal electronic notebook or wiki should be sufficient. (My teams use Word for detailed specs and OneNote for other documentation.)

Bugs

In traditional Waterfall, features might not be validated until months after implementation. On a large project with hundreds of engineers, validation may find thousands of bugs. Often, validation takes as long as or longer than implementation.

Over the years, traditional Waterfall teams have devised a variety of ways to handle large bug counts:

- With limited time to fix so many bugs, each bug must be prioritized and duplicate bug reports removed. At Microsoft, we call this process "bug triage." Team leaders representing each job role meet for roughly an hour each day and review every new or updated active bug. They discuss the impact of the bug (severity, frequency, and percentage of customers affected) and set an appropriate priority (fix now, fix before release, fix if time, or fix in subsequent release). They can also decide that the bug is a duplicate of a prior reported issue or that the bug isn't worth fixing (usually because a trivial workaround is available, most customers won't encounter the bug, or the fix would cause more havoc than the bug).

- Some teams have "bug jail," in which individual engineers must stop further development and only resolve bugs until their individual bug counts drop below a reasonable level (such as below five bugs each).

- Some teams have something like "workaholic Wednesdays"—one day a week when the team doesn't go home until all bugs are resolved, or at least brought below a reasonable level (such as below five bugs per engineer).

- Every traditional Waterfall team I've encountered has substantial stabilization periods at the end of each milestone or at the end of each release. During stabilization, the team (and often the entire organization) focuses on nothing but fixing bugs, doing various forms of system validation, and logging any new or reoccurring bugs they find. Stabilization for a large project can sometimes last longer than all the specification, implementation, and prestabilization validation times put together.

- Some progressive development teams might employ extensive code reviews, inspections, unit testing, static analysis, pair programming, and even test-driven development (TDD) during implementation to reduce the number of bugs found during validation. These methods make a big difference, but you are usually still left with a substantial number of bugs at the end, partially because system validation happens well after implementation, and partially because adherence to these practices varies widely among developers.

In Kanban, a bug's life is a bit different:

- Kanban's small batches ensure that validation happens only days after implementation, so bug backlogs are small and fixes are readily apparent.

- Kanban ensures that every task implemented has been through code review, inspected, unit tested, statically analyzed, pair programmed, or designed and verified using TDD, based on the implementation done rule that the team imposed on itself. Even reckless developers are kept in line by their own teams. (No one likes cleaning up after a lazy slob.) This further reduces bug counts.

- Likewise, the validation done rule ensures that every task has gone through integration testing and all its issues are resolved. Thus, by the time a task is done with validation, it's ready for production use. I talk about taking advantage of this fact in Chapter 6, "Deploying components, apps, and services."

Even though every work item completing validation each day has gone through integration testing and all its issues are resolved, bugs can still be discovered in production use, stress testing, security testing, usability and beta testing, and a variety of other product-wide system testing. However, the stabilization period required to fix those issues is far shorter, and in my experience, the number of stabilization bugs opened per feature team drops from hundreds to 10 to 20 (a couple of weeks of effort to resolve).

After adapting to Kanban, traditional Waterfall teams might choose to continue bug triage, bug jail, workaholic Wednesdays, and long stabilization periods. However, teams may soon find some or all of those practices unnecessary. In a large organization, a cross-team, product-wide triage stabilization period might still be needed (see Chapter 7), but individual teams using Kanban won't have enough bugs to make team triage, bug jail, or workaholic Wednesdays useful.

Engaging with customers

Traditional Waterfall teams typically engage with customers during planning (before work on the release begins), every one to six months at the end of stabilization for each milestone (perhaps as part of a preview program), and during final release stabilization (often as part of a beta program).

As experienced engineers know, customer feedback is invaluable for specifying, implementing, and validating product improvements. Customer engagement with traditional Waterfall teams is limited because the product is usually too buggy or incomplete to use. Customers can't provide actionable feedback when they can't use the product. Instead, customers must wait until the end of stabilization periods, when the product has the fewest-known bugs.

In contrast, Kanban provides an opportunity to engage with customers at whatever cadence the team or its customers finds most convenient, including continuously with customers who are onsite. Kanban enables this because when a task is through validation, it's ready for production use.

Naturally, you want to try out product improvements with a limited number of customers first, and gauge their reactions, before publishing those improvements to your entire customer base. One common approach is to first have the entire product development team try the latest version, then share it through an early adopter program, then publish it to a broader preview audience, and then finally release it to all your customers. (I describe an example in the following "Inside Xbox" section.)

The customer feedback you get along the way can be used to hold back changes that don't work, adjust designs, reorder pending work, find subtle or rare bugs, fill gaps in usability scenarios, and expand features in areas that customers love. Since Kanban limits work in progress (small batches), it's easy to adjust to customer input within days.

To take advantage of the customer feedback opportunity, you need to establish a preview program, an early adopter program, and a way for the entire product development team to try the latest version. Here are some possibilities:

- Many traditional Waterfall teams have beta programs already. You can repurpose your beta program as a preview program.

- To establish an early adopter program, you can engage the most active members of your beta audience or hand-select key customers and offer them early adopter status as a perk.

- To expose the entire product team to the latest builds, follow the steps I outline in Chapter 6.

Soon, you'll be enjoying greater confidence, higher quality and usability, and more delighted customers. There's nothing quite like engaged customers providing actionable feedback on working products.

The last, and arguably most critical, step to ensure that your team and your management commit to Kanban is to measure the great results you're getting, and then celebrate your success. That's the topic of the next section.

Inside Xbox

Xbox One launched in the fall of 2013, and at the time of this writing has shipped new releases of the platform every month since. The Xbox One product team uses a variety of methodologies: Scrum, Scrummerfall (traditional Waterfall with short, fixed-length milestones called "sprints"), variants of Extreme Programming (XP), and Kanban. All of these techniques enable frequent customer feedback.

The move to monthly releases had its challenges, but was surprisingly smooth and natural. In hindsight, I feel that two key changes made this smooth transition possible:

- Roughly 18 months in advance, we synchronized all enterprise Scrum and Scrummerfall sprints and XP iterations to match a shared 4-week cadence. Kanban releases continuously and can match any cadence, so the Kanban teams didn't need to adjust.

- In the months leading up to the launch, we released new platform builds to the Xbox product team weekly, then to the early adopter program the week after, and then to a preview audience monthly. We released fixes immediately for issues found by each audience. Once Xbox One launched, we simply continued that release cadence and approach, adding a broad release to all customers a few weeks after the preview audience received it.

- Establishing the various release audiences was pretty easy, relatively speaking.

- We already had a release mechanism for the weekly Xbox product team builds. It's called "dog food" (as in "eating our own dog food"), and has been around since the first version of the Xbox. Naturally, we needed to update the program for Xbox One, but that was anticipated.

- We already had a passionate early adopter program. Basically, we ask all full-time Microsoft employees if they're interested in early releases of Xbox—first come, first served. The list fills within hours. Again, we needed to update our deployment process for Xbox One, but that was expected.

- And we already had a passionate Xbox beta audience that we could convert over to Xbox One preview. This was the most work—not to get the audience, but to reconfigure the beta feedback site, logistics, and tooling to a monthly release cadence.

- Now that Xbox is releasing once a month, we never want to go back. Our customers love the new features and responsiveness to requests. Our engineers love the predictability, the decreased churn between releases, and the reduced pressure (if your feature misses one month, it can always go out the next). And our management loves the positive press we've received and how that's translated to the bottom line.

Celebrating performance improvements

Even if your traditional Waterfall team takes easily to Kanban and likes the change, members may still question whether the change was worth it. After all, traditional Waterfall does work, and has likely worked for years. Your management probably has a similar concern: Was the effort to adopt Kanban worth the cost?

While each team has its own reasons, you likely adopted Kanban to increase agility and deliver more high-quality value to your customers in less time. The good news is that it's straightforward to measure those outcomes. By measuring them from the start, and showing your team and management how your results improve over time, you'll enhance everyone's commitment to the change and boost morale and team pride in the process.

I'll focus on two daily measurements and their moving averages to capture agility, productivity, and quality. I selected these particular measures—completed tasks and unresolved bugs—because they are easy to calculate for both Waterfall and Kanban, they have clear definitions, and they relate directly to agility, productivity, and quality. Here's a breakdown of each measure:

	Completed tasks	Unresolved bugs
Definition	Count of the team's tasks that completed validation that day with all issues resolved	Count of the team's unresolved bugs that day
Concept measured	Day-to-day agility	Day-to-day bug debt
Moving average captures	Productivity	Product quality
Waterfall calculation	Count the rough number of the team's tasks in each spec that completed validation and had all issues resolved by the end of a milestone or release, and associate that count with the end date of the respective milestone or release.	Extract the number of the team's unresolved bugs by day from your bug-tracking system.
Kanban calculation	Count the number of the team's tasks that completed the done rules for validation on each date.	Extract the number of the team's unresolved bugs by day from your bug-tracking system.
Caveats	Only measures productivity of task completion, not other daily activities or tasks without specifications.	Only measures aspects of product quality captured in bugs, but doesn't account for different types of bugs.

Notes on these measures:

- If the size of your team varies dramatically, you should divide by the number of team members, resulting in completed tasks per team member and unresolved bugs per team member. Doing so makes the measures easier to compare across teams but less intuitive to management, in my experience.

- The completed tasks calculation for Waterfall bulks all the tasks at the end of each milestone or release because that's the earliest date when the tasks are known to be validated with all issues resolved. However, if your Waterfall team associates all bugs directly with tasks, you can count tasks toward the day when their last bug was resolved. Getting this extra accuracy is nice, but it isn't essential. In particular, the extra accuracy doesn't matter for the moving average (the productivity measure), so long as you average over the length of your milestones.

- The moving average can be a 7-day average for measuring weekly productivity, a 30-day average for monthly productivity, or whatever length you want. To compare the productivity of Waterfall to Kanban, you should average over the length of your Waterfall milestones.

Figure 4-1 and Figure 4-2 are examples of plots of completed tasks and unresolved bugs over four nine-week periods (included in a downloadable worksheet; see the book's introduction for more details). The first two periods are Waterfall milestones, split into six weeks of implementation and three weeks of validation. The second two periods are Kanban running continuously. The data is based on the team configuration I used as an example in Chapter 3, "Hitting deadlines." I have the team working seven days a week (for simplicity, not punishment). Their pace of task work remains the same throughout all four periods, which is artificial but unbiased. (I do add a little random noise throughout to make the results a bit more realistic.)

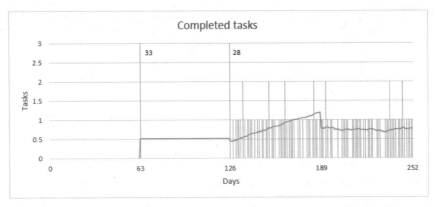

FIGURE 4-1 Plot of completed tasks over four nine-week periods, with a superimposed running average.

Looking at the chart of completed tasks, all tasks are considered completed on the final day of validation during the first two Waterfall periods. The two columns of completed tasks from those periods go about 10 times the height of the chart. I've zoomed in to better view the nine-week moving average line measuring productivity. It starts at around 0.52 tasks per day (33 tasks / 63 days), increases to around 1.2 tasks per day as the results from the second Waterfall milestone combine with the Kanban results, and then settles to around 0.76 tasks per day as the steady stream of Kanban work establishes itself.

The improvement from 0.52 to 0.76 represents a 46 percent increase in productivity. That's the equivalent to working five days and getting seven and a half days of tasks completed—it's like you worked hard through the weekend and still got the weekend off. The day-to-day agility of Kanban is also immediately apparent, as work is completed daily instead of being delivered in bulk.

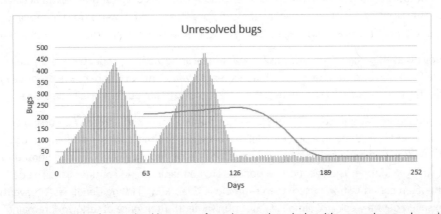

FIGURE 4-2 Plot of unresolved bugs over four nine-week periods, with a superimposed running average.

The unresolved bugs chart in Figure 4-2 displays a fairly typical Waterfall pattern of building up a bug backlog during the six-week implementation phase of the milestone and then resolving those bugs during the three-week validation phase. This shows as the two inverted V shapes, one for each

Waterfall milestone. This simple example has a fairly uniform bug resolution rate during validation. In practice, bug resolution rates often fluctuate significantly as complicated issues are uncovered and some fixes regress old problems.

Once the Kanban period starts, there is a fairly steady stream of unresolved bugs, but it never builds up. Bugs are kept in check by the WIP limits and done rules. As a result, the nine-week moving average line measuring quality improves dramatically with Kanban. The product is always ready for production use and customer feedback.

Seeing these dramatic improvements in productivity and quality should be enough to warm the hearts of hardened cynics and skeptical managers. Sharing them weekly with your team and your management gives you all something to celebrate (in addition to the increased customer value you deliver).

What's more, with Kanban, the quality level is steady throughout the product cycle, so the prolonged stabilization periods associated with traditional Waterfall are gone or, in large organizations, reduced to only two or three weeks of system-wide testing. Replacing months of stabilization with a few weeks at most yields more time for continuous product enhancements, making the measurable improvements in productivity and quality even more remarkable.

However, a month or two will pass before you begin to see great results. The cynics and skeptics on your team are bound to have questions. It's time for the rude Q & A.

Rude Q & A

What follows is a rude Q & A session that is based on questions I've received from traditional Waterfall team members when they were introduced to Kanban. I hope it covers many of the questions you receive.

Q   Why are we adopting Kanban?

A   The software industry continues to evolve. Customers now expect their apps and services to update automatically and be improved continuously. Our current practices impede us from keeping pace.

Q   Instead, how about we stop changing practices, plans, and requirements constantly?

A   Plans and requirements always change, no matter how well prepared or well considered they are. Even when you are your own customer, you constantly change your mind. Nevertheless, stable plans, requirements, and practices aren't sufficient for us to react quickly to the current market.

Q   So you're saying it's hopeless?

A   It's not hopeless at all. The rest of the industry is moving forward. We can join in with some relatively small changes that have a big impact.

Q   Will we need training for Kanban?

A   We'll learn Kanban mostly from doing it every day. Books about Kanban and Kanban coaches are available to help us with adoption.

Q   Are you going to make me sit in a cubical farm or share a desk?

A   No, you don't have to change offices or share desks. You don't even have to change how you write specs, software, or tests. We're just adding a daily standup meeting at which we track our workflow on a large board.

Q   How is adding another meeting going to make me faster?

A   The daily standup lasts less than 15 minutes and replaces our old planning and status meetings. We'll schedule it at a convenient time for the whole team. Regardless, it's smooth and continuous workflow that makes the team faster.

Q   How do we get smooth and continuous workflow?

A   Today, we specify, implement, and validate features in bulk. It's fast, but when a plan or requirement changes, we lose work and momentum, and when bugs are found late, we have lots of costly rework. Going forward, we'll pace specification, implementation, and validation to run at similar rates so that we can smoothly complete small batches continuously.

Q   How do small batches make us faster?

A   Small batches speed us up in a variety of ways:

- When a plan or requirement changes, it affects only a small batch, so less work is wasted and the team can adjust quickly.

- Small batches mean smaller bug backlogs, so we don't need dedicated team stabilization periods.

- We have to specify, implement, and validate only a small batch at a time, so we don't write specs that aren't implemented, implement code that isn't validated, or write tests that are never run.

- We can get customer feedback after every small batch, which avoids being blindsided later and reworking major portions of the design (or releasing a product that customers dislike).

In all, small batches significantly reduce wasted effort and rework, while improving the quality of our product.

Q   So why haven't we been using small batches all along?

A   Small batches require a coordinated flow of work. If analysts specify more features in a week than developers can implement, specifications start piling up, and you're back to doing work in bulk. Likewise for developers implementing more features than testers can validate. If you can't pace specification, implementation, and validation to run at similar rates, you're stuck working in bulk and dealing with wasted effort, large bug backlogs, and substantial rework.

Q We have a wide variety of analysts, developers, and testers. How do you pace work properly?

A You limit the pace of specification, implementation, and validation to match one another. You base those work limits on the current pace of each step, plus some buffer to account for the variety of people and work involved. These work limits are often called "work-in-progress (WIP) limits." Naturally, your initial guesses about the limits will need fine-tuning, but even initial guesses are typically good enough to produce a smoother, more continuous flow of small batches.

Q Wouldn't limiting work make us slower?

A We're not limiting people, we're limiting the kinds of work they do. If developers are stuck on a feature, an analyst specifying more features doesn't help. Instead, the analyst should work to unblock the developers (for example, clarify the spec, escalate an issue, research a customer preference, or bring in partner expertise). By focusing on keeping the work flowing smoothly, and limiting work so that it maintains a smooth pace, we actually get more work done in less time.

Q Why not keep the analyst working and have the developer move on to the next task?

A The key is the status of the blocked implementation task:

- If the task is blocked by an external dependency, the developer should move on to the next task until the old task is unblocked. We'll keep an eye on the blocked task in a special column on the signboard.

- If the task is blocked by a design question or issue, it's the analyst's responsibility to unblock the task, ideally while the issue is still fresh in the developer's mind. The limits on work and the visibility of blocked tasks prevent analysts from ignoring design issues and letting them fester.

The same applies for blocked specification and validation tasks. Instead of letting problems pile up, we're going to work together to fix them quickly. That keeps work flowing smoothly, fixes issues before they permeate the product and become harder to repair, and delivers value faster and more continuously to our customers.

Q Won't I be constantly hassled about fixing problems?

A Actually, you'll be hassled less than you are today. That's because we always have problems, but today we find and fix them late. By fixing problems early, they are fresh in your mind, easier to fix, and don't have time to multiply and cause further trouble. You will be hassled earlier than before, but most folks appreciate the dividends of not having problems fester.

Q Will everyone be coming to me with problems?

A No, you'll work on individual tasks like you always have. We're adding a daily standup meeting where we track our workflow on a large board. That signboard will show your work, and everyone else's work, on cards that flow across the three steps: Specify, Implement, and Validate. The WIP limits that set the right pacing will be written above each step on the signboard. Everyone will see when work is getting blocked and bunched up—they won't all just come to you. Instead, the team will work out issues together.

Q What if one person keeps causing all the blockage?

A There's a classic remedy if someone really can't do his or her job. However, if someone is careless or lazy and tends to pass on half-done work, he won't get away with it. We're going to have done rules for Specify, Implement, and Validate. Before someone can move a card, claiming it's done with the current step, the work has to pass the done rules for that step. No half-done work is allowed.

Q Who determines the done rules?

A You and the rest of the team decide on the done rules you'll follow. You know what causes issues. You know how to do your job well. You get to decide when a task should be considered done. Once the team decides on the rules, we'll write them at the bottom of the signboard so that there's no confusion. Anytime the rules need adjustment, we can change them together.

Q What else changes with Kanban?

A Nothing—that's it until we want to improve even further. For now, we'll have a daily standup in front of a big board with our work steps written on it, cards showing our work, limits on the number of cards at each step, and rules at the bottom of the signboard that determine when a card is done with its current step. Whenever you're done with a step, based on the done rules, you'll move your card on the signboard and grab the next available card. If no cards are available, that indicates that workflow is blocked, and you should work with your teammates to unblock the flow.

Q Where will the cards come from?

A We'll take our current feature list and work backlog, write the items on cards, bucket them in priority order, and place them on the left side of the signboard, in front of the specification step. When new work arrives or plans change, we'll add and rearrange cards as needed. (Details in Chapter 3, "Hitting deadlines," and Chapter 7, "Using Kanban within large organizations.")

Q When a card moves from one step to the next, who works on it?

A We'll assign work to whomever is free and capable of doing that work at the time. Pretty much like we do today, but as needed, not planned far in advance.

Q We have daily standups in front of a board that tracks progress. Are we already doing Kanban?

A Many traditional Waterfall teams meet daily in front of a board that's used to track progress. However, it's not Kanban unless you list your steps on the board (like specification, implementation, and verification), and each step has a work-in-progress (WIP) limit, a Done column, and a done rule clearly marked on the board.

Q Why does each step need its own Done column?

A Say you just completed implementing an item (it passes the implementation done rule). Without an implementation-specific check mark or implementation Done column, how would you indicate that the item is ready for validation? On an ordinary board, you just move the item to validation. However, that means the item is actively being validated and counts toward the validation WIP limit—neither of which is true. What's worse is that the item no longer counts toward the implementation WIP limit, so you're free to implement another item, even if validation is over-whelmed and needs help. The Done column for each step clearly indicates the status of each item and controls the flow of items in conjunction with their WIP limits.

Q What happens to milestones with Kanban?

A The larger project might have release milestones to sync across teams, but we no longer need them as an individual team. Our small batches are always complete and ready for production use, based on our validation done rules. Learn more in Chapter 7, "Using Kanban within large organizations."

Q What about stabilization?

A The larger project might have release stabilization to resolve system-wide issues, but we no longer need it as an individual team. Our done rules ensure that work is done at the end of each step, with no remaining issues to stabilize.

Q If other project teams are using Waterfall, won't they still need stabilization?

A Yes, they will. While other teams stabilize, we can do a few different things:

- We can keep working on new tasks for the current project milestone. This might upset Waterfall folks or break project rules, so it may not be an option.

- We can work on new tasks for the next project milestone and check them in to a different source control branch.

- We can improve infrastructure and tooling and address other technical debt that has been neglected.

- We can train ourselves on new techniques and methods.

- We can determine the root cause of various issues we've encountered and seek to fix them.

- We can help other teams stabilize their code, particularly teams we depend on. This option may not be the most alluring, but it's the most helpful.

- We can run innovative experiments and acquire customer feedback.

Q What happens to planning?

A We'll still participate in overall release and project planning, but our team planning is simply a matter of ordering cards on our big board. We'll save a great deal of time and produce more value at higher quality, while easily and quickly adjusting to plan and requirement changes.

Q It sounds pretty simple. Aren't there sprints and burndowns or something?

A No, there's no unfamiliar terminology or new ways of doing the work. Kanban is pretty simple and direct. Kanban roughly means "signal card," "sign," "board," or "looking at the board." It refers to the cards that represent our work, the signboard displaying our workflow steps (and their assigned WIP limits and done rules), and our daily standup when we look at the signboard. There's nothing more to it. We keep working on new cards within the WIP limits we've set, ensure that the cards are done with each step, and then work on the next cards. If cards start piling up, we figure out what's wrong and fix it so that work continues to flow smoothly and value is delivered continuously to our customers. It's a fast, simple, and easy way to work.

Checklist

Here's a checklist of actions for your team members to adapt from Waterfall:

- ❏ Explain why a change is necessary.

- ❏ Reassure team members that they can do their work as they did before, without learning new roles or unfamiliar terminology.

- ❏ Introduce daily standups that are attended by the entire feature team.

- ❏ Describe why it's important to work on features in small batches.

- ❏ Decide which features will require formal specification documents and which can be specified informally with whiteboard photos and notes.

- ❏ Determine how lower bug backlogs should affect bug-management and stabilization periods.

- ❏ Arrange opportunities for frequent customer feedback on the continuous value added to your products.

- ❏ Perform the actions listed in the checklist in Chapter 2, "Kanban quick-start guide."

- ❏ Measure completed tasks and unresolved bugs, or whatever productivity and quality metrics you choose, on a regular basis.

- ❏ Celebrate productivity and quality improvement (as well as continuous delivery of value to customers).

- ❏ Answer any questions team members have with respect and appreciation for their past accomplishments.

CHAPTER 5

Evolving from Scrum

This chapter is for people currently using Scrum for product development. If you don't use Scrum, feel free to skip this chapter.

Kanban will seem quite familiar to people with Scrum experience—using Kanban is a straight-forward evolution. Daily standup meetings, working together in feature teams, completing features before starting new ones, and engaging frequently with customers are all common practices in both approaches. Roles like Scrum Master and Product Owner are welcome in Kanban but aren't as prescribed as in Scrum.

After more than 20 years of using traditional Waterfall, I spent 8 years using Scrum, and I loved every minute. Scrum was a revelation to me—the iteration, the focus on empowering teams, the intimate customer connection, and the agility were all breakthrough benefits. If you'd like to learn more about Scrum, I recommend Ken Schwaber's classic book, *Agile Project Management with Scrum* (Microsoft Press, 2004).

Scrum is an enormous improvement over the traditional Waterfall approach. I'd still be using Scrum today if Corey Ladas, the guy who introduced me to Scrum in 2003, hadn't shown me how he used Kanban at Corbis in 2007. (Corey and David Anderson were kind enough to give me a full introduction to the methods they used at Corbis.) It took me three and a half years to find the right opportunity and courage to use Kanban to evolve my Scrum Teams, and then I was hooked. Scrum is fantastic, but Kanban is as close to project-management nirvana as I've ever experienced. With Kanban, every minute of work is spent directly adding customer value—nothing seems wasted.

> **Note** For those who seek to understand the hows and whys of Kanban in more detail, or want to consider a bridge between Scrum and Kanban, I recommend Corey Ladas's book, *Scrumban: Essays on Kanban Systems for Lean Software Development* (Modus Cooperandi, 2009).

This chapter is devoted to helping Scrum Team members evolve to using Kanban without much fuss or hassle. I've included a rude Q & A listing questions that a blunt team member might ask, followed by pragmatic answers meant to reassure, build trust in the new approach, and clearly explain how to achieve great results with Kanban.

The topics covered are:

Introducing Kanban to a Scrum Team
Mapping the roles and terms
Evolving the events
Celebrating performance improvements
Rude Q & A
Checklist

Introducing Kanban to a Scrum Team

A Scrum Team is already familiar with agile project management. If team members previously used traditional Waterfall, they may have great reverence for Scrum and its benefits (although some may miss the structure and the separation of disciplines in Waterfall). Scrum is an effective incremental technique for quickly delivering high-quality products to customers.

However, the time-boxing of Scrum sprints enforces artificial boundaries on plan changes, customer feedback, release dates, and process improvements. Ideally, teams could handle those events at any time, but Scrum ties them to the planning at the beginning of sprints, or review and retrospective events at the end of sprints. This timing avoids the interruption of work during a sprint, but it leads to delays in plan adjustments, feedback, releases, and improvements and adds extra events. Kanban removes the artificial sprint boundaries and the additional events while keeping the workflow smooth and uninterrupted.

In addition, Scrum introduces a number of special terms that may be unfamiliar and confusing to new team members, including sprint, increment, Daily Scrum, Product Backlog, Sprint Backlog, Scrum Master, and Product Owner. These terms can increase the difficulty new team members might have acclimating and becoming productive quickly. With Kanban, you can use whatever terms and roles are familiar to your team, which eases the effort of bringing new people onboard and getting them to work effectively.

Regardless of the advantages, people may resist evolving from Scrum by using Kanban. Instead of treating Kanban as an overhaul or as a radical shift from Scrum, I recommend that you acknowledge how beneficial and effective Scrum is and introduce Kanban as the next iteration on Scrum's agility. With all the qualities that Scrum and Kanban have in common, many adjustments will seem like refinements. Your team should adapt quickly using the initial Kanban enhancements and may find the reduced overhead and improved productivity to be surprising. Once the team masters the use of Kanban, it can choose to improve further by making more significant modifications to its approach.

When a Scrum Team evolves by using Kanban, reassure team members by saying something like, "Scrum has proven itself to be an effective, incremental approach to rapidly deliver high-quality products to our customers. We want to take the next iteration forward, while keeping our existing roles and workflow steps. We'll reduce our planning events, detect and correct flow issues immediately, and be more explicit about how we define what it means for each step of our work to be done. The changes will be visible on the big board we use to track our work. In addition to displaying our backlog, the board will now separate in-progress and completed work items for each step, display our done rules for each step, and have limits for how much work should be in progress for each step. While these changes might seem cosmetic, the work-in-progress (WIP) limits and done rules will catch issues early and enable a continuous flow of work—one continuous sprint. We'll reduce time spent in Sprint Planning and always have production-ready code to share with customers."

At this point, you can proceed to the Kanban quick-start guide (Chapter 2), using your current backlog of work as a starting point. But before you move on, here are a few points about the rest of this chapter:

- Experienced Scrum Team members will likely wonder what happens to the various Scrum roles and events in the evolution to Kanban. I cover these topics in the next two sections: "Mapping the roles and terms" and "Evolving the events."

- To show your management and your team how Kanban is improving productivity and quality, you'll want to measure and celebrate your progress. This can be critical to gain commitment to Kanban, it's easy, and it provides a nice morale boost. See the "Celebrating performance improvements" section.

- Your Scrum Team members are sure to have questions about Kanban, so I've included answers to common questions in the "Rude Q & A" section.

Inside Xbox

A few years ago, I moved two experienced Scrum Teams to Kanban after we had resolved larger issues around stable builds, stable environments, and frequent, reliable deployments to production. I introduced Kanban to my Scrum Teams as another kind of improvement. Two of my teams agreed to try it, starting with a two-month trial period.

The only complaint during adoption came from one of the longtime Microsoft team members. He preferred the formality of monthly planning events, but the rest of the Scrum Team didn't. They compromised by being a bit more formal in their specifications.

Overall, team members found Kanban straightforward and simple. The teams were already using a whiteboard to track their sprint tasks, so Kanban amounted to adding Done columns, done rules, and WIP limits to the existing board. They welcomed the reduction in the number of events and had little trouble adjusting to the WIP limits.

I attended some of the first standup meetings with each team and answered any questions that arose. Each team saw a need for a breakdown step before implementation and validation. (I've since recommended that all my teams include breakdown as part of their Specify step.) After the first few weeks, the teams were accustomed to Kanban and rarely had questions.

Once the two-month trial period was over, both Scrum Teams reported that they loved Kanban and wanted to keep using it. Kanban has since spread to other nearby teams, long after I moved to a new group.

Mapping the roles and terms

In addition to the Development Team, Scrum codifies two crucial roles: Scrum Master and Product Owner. You can keep these roles when you use Kanban or spread some of their responsibilities across the team. In this section, I'll map Scrum roles and Scrum terms to the roles and terms mentioned in Chapter 2, "Kanban quick-start guide."

In Scrum, the Scrum Master enables the team to deliver value to customers. The Scrum Master facilitates events, ensures the customer representative (the Product Owner) works effectively with the team and the Product Backlog, coaches and empowers the team, removes impediments to progress, engages in Scrum efforts across the larger organization, and otherwise does everything possible to ensure that the team incrementally delivers a high-quality, usable product to customers while keeping progress up to date and visible to everyone involved.

When using Kanban (and modern versions of Scrum), the entire team is actively involved in removing barriers and doing everything possible to incrementally deliver a high-quality, usable product to customers while keeping progress up to date and visible to everyone *directly* involved. In Kanban, the team's project manager is responsible for sharing that progress with those *indirectly* involved, such as leadership and the larger organization. Every team member is encouraged to frequently engage with customers, although analysts are primarily responsible for keeping the customer close to heart, whether or not there is a single customer representative (a single Product Owner).

> **Tip** Personally, I love my customers like family. Sometimes they are frustrating and difficult, like family, but I love them anyway. Without customers, our teams wouldn't exist. If we keep our customers in our hearts and have real empathy for who they are, we'll create better products and see our love returned. Mushy, but true.

Kanban involves every team member through the use of the signboard, note cards, WIP limits, and done rules. Since there is one continuous sprint, there is only one backlog to manage and every note card is an increment on delivered customer value. The note cards in the signboard's backlog represent user stories, features, scenarios, use cases, or other kinds of work items. In the first step (Specify, in my examples), large work items can be broken down (decomposed) into smaller tasks, each with its own note card.

Team members move the note cards themselves, keeping progress up to date and visible to the team and to customers when they drop by. The WIP limits expose problems immediately, so team members can respond anytime during the day or at the daily standup. In addition to Scrum's definition of done for completed work items, Kanban uses done rules at each step along the way to ensure a high-quality, usable product at all times for customers.

When you evolve from Scrum by using Kanban, you can keep your current Scrum Masters and Product Owners. Over time, you can divide the duties of those roles among different team members the way you want.

- You can engage leadership and partners separately from customers (in the same way that project managers are described separately from analysts in Chapter 2).

- You can involve more customers than a single Product Owner.

- You can focus individuals on service delivery or other specific needs of your team.

- You can leave your roles exactly as they are today.

In Kanban, you can choose how to manage the roles on your team. The key is to keep value flowing smoothly to your customers so that they can provide you with the timely feedback you need to keep your products desirable and competitive.

Evolving the events

Scrum establishes several regular events. In the following table, I describe each event and how that event is replaced in Kanban.

Scrum event	Description	Frequency	Kanban replacement	Frequency
High-level planning	The Product Owner establishes the initial Product Backlog of work.	Once a project, or perhaps quarterly for a service	Similar exercise with key stakeholders (see Chapter 3).	Once a project, or perhaps quarterly for a service
Sprint Planning	The Product Owner collaborates with the Development Team to select the highest-priority items from the Product Backlog for the upcoming sprint.	At the beginning of each sprint	No event—items pulled from the backlog in order as needed.	N/A
Daily Scrum	Each team member answers the following questions: What have you done since the last Scrum? What will you do before the next Scrum? What impediments stand in the way?	Daily	Standup meeting, but only the question about impediments is asked after viewing the signboard, and only those who are blocked answer.	Daily
Sprint Review	The Scrum Team presents the completed, working software to stakeholders for feedback.	At the end of each sprint	No event—customers see the latest product daily or whenever they desire to do so.	N/A
Sprint Retrospective	The team discusses process improvements for the next sprint.	At the end of each sprint	No event—flow issues are apparent and fixed daily.	N/A

Notice that both Scrum and Kanban have high-level planning and a daily standup meeting, but Kanban forgoes Scrum's other events in favor of smooth workflow and continuous product delivery.

A few details are worth noting:

- Sometimes work items are broken down into smaller tasks during the Sprint Planning event. In Kanban, my teams do this breakdown during the Specify step.

- Some Scrum Teams also use the Sprint Planning event to assign work items. Work-item assignment in Kanban is deferred until a note card is ready to move from one step to the next on the signboard.

- It's not necessary to ask "What have you done?" and "What will you do?" at the daily standup meetings in Kanban because that status is displayed on the signboard at all times.

- Because Kanban continuously delivers a production-ready product, customers can see the latest improvements quickly and provide their feedback (either directly or through usage patterns). There's no requirement for a regular Sprint Review event. However, a Kanban team might still choose to hold regular or special presentations to highlight compelling features or to get feedback on design decisions.

- No regular Sprint Retrospective event is required because Kanban's WIP limits and done rules will block tasks immediately if breakdowns in workflow or quality occur. However, other subtle or surprising issues may arise that disrupt quality or workflow. When that happens, Kanban teams should discuss the issues in depth and drive improvements to their product, tools, and approach, just as they did as Scrum Teams.

Celebrating performance improvements

Even if your Scrum Team takes easily to Kanban and likes the change, members might still question whether the change was worth it. After all, Scrum is terrific and has many similarities to Kanban. Your management probably has a similar concern: Was the effort to evolve by using Kanban worth the cost? (Note that this section is quite similar to the same-titled section in Chapter 4, "Adapting from Waterfall." I've adapted the data and measurements to Scrum.)

While each team has its own reasons, you likely evolved by using Kanban to increase agility and deliver more high-quality value to your customers in less time. The good news is that measuring those outcomes is straightforward. By measuring them from the start, and showing your team and management how your results improve over time, you'll enhance everyone's commitment to the change and boost morale and team pride in the process.

I'll focus on two daily measurements and their moving averages to capture agility, productivity, and quality. I selected these particular measures—completed tasks and unresolved bugs—because they are easy to calculate for Scrum and Kanban, they have clear definitions, and they relate directly to agility, productivity, and quality. Here's a breakdown of each measure:

	Completed tasks	**Unresolved bugs**
Definition	Count of the team's tasks that completed validation that day with all issues resolved.	Count of the team's unresolved bugs that day.
Concept measured	Day-to-day agility	Day-to-day bug debt
Moving average captures	Productivity	Product quality
Scrum calculation	Count the rough number of the team's tasks in each work item that completed validation and had all issues resolved by the end of each sprint, and associate that count with the end date of the respective sprint.	Extract the number of the team's unresolved bugs by day from your bug-tracking system.
Kanban calculation	Count the number of the team's tasks that completed the done rules for validation on each date.	Extract the number of the team's unresolved bugs by day from your bug-tracking system.
Caveats	Only measures productivity of task completion, not other daily activities.	Only measures aspects of product quality captured in bugs, but doesn't account for different types of bugs.

Notes on these measures:

- If the size of your team varies dramatically, you should divide by the number of team members, resulting in completed tasks per team member and unresolved bugs per team member. Doing so makes the measures easier to compare across teams but less intuitive to management, in my experience.

- The completed tasks calculation for Scrum bulks all the tasks at the end of each sprint because that's the earliest date when the tasks are known to be validated with all issues resolved. However, if your Scrum Team associates all bugs directly with tasks, you can count tasks toward the day when their last bug was resolved. Getting this extra accuracy is nice, but it isn't essential. In particular, the extra accuracy doesn't matter for the moving average (the productivity measure), so long as you average over the length of your sprints.

- The moving average can be a 7-day average for measuring weekly productivity, a 30-day average for monthly productivity, or whatever length you want. To compare the productivity of Scrum to Kanban, you should average over the length of your sprints.

Figure 5-1 and Figure 5-2 are examples of plots of completed tasks and unresolved bugs over four four-week periods (included in a downloadable worksheet; see the book's introduction for details). The first two periods are 28-day Scrum sprints. The second two periods reflect Kanban running continuously. The data is based on the team configuration I used as an example in Chapter 3, "Hitting deadlines." I have the team working seven days a week (for simplicity, not punishment). Their pace of task work remains the same throughout all four periods, which is artificial but unbiased. (I do add a little random noise throughout to make the results a bit more realistic.)

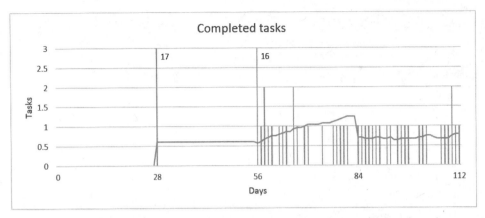

FIGURE 5-1 Plot of completed tasks over four four-week periods, with a superimposed running average.

Looking at the chart of completed tasks, all tasks are considered complete on the final day of the sprint during the first Scrum sprints. The two columns of completed tasks from those periods go about six times the height of the chart. I've zoomed in to better view the four-week moving average line measuring productivity. It starts at around 0.61 tasks per day (17 tasks / 28 days), increases to around 1.2 tasks per day as the results from the second sprint combine with the Kanban results, and then settles to around 0.76 tasks per day as the steady stream of Kanban work establishes itself.

Note Scrum enthusiasts may notice that the Waterfall productivity number from Chapter 4 was 0.52, and the Scrum productivity number is only 17 percent higher at 0.61. In practice, the productivity of Scrum can be far higher than Waterfall (although 17 percent is still a nice improvement). However, my Waterfall example is idealized in a few ways: the milestones are short (nine weeks), the bug debt is nearly completely paid off at the end of each milestone (often not the case), and I didn't count the prolonged stabilization period that Waterfall typically has after the last milestone.

The improvement from 0.61 to 0.76 represents a 25 percent increase in productivity. That's the equivalent of working five days and completing six and a quarter days of tasks—more than an extra day a week without working weekends. The day-to-day agility of Kanban is also immediately apparent, as work is completed daily instead of being delivered in bulk each sprint.

The unresolved bugs chart in Figure 5-2 displays a fairly typical sprint pattern of building up a bug backlog somewhat during a sprint and then resolving those bugs at the end. This shows as the two inverted V shapes, one for each sprint. Note that far fewer bugs build up during Scrum sprints versus the Waterfall implementation periods shown in Chapter 4. Part of that is due to the shorter sprints, and part is the result of the Scrum Team's effort to catch bugs early.

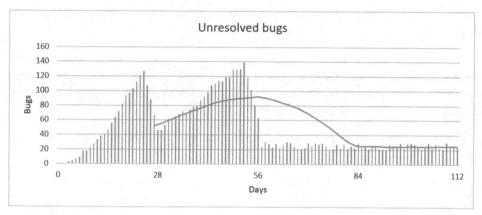

FIGURE 5-2 Plot of unresolved bugs over four four-week periods, with a superimposed running average.

Seeing these improvements in productivity and quality should be enough to warm the hearts of hardened cynics and skeptical managers. Sharing them weekly with your team and your management gives you all something to celebrate (in addition to the increased customer value you deliver).

However, a month or two will pass before you begin to see great results. The cynics and skeptics on your team are bound to have questions. It's time for the rude Q & A.

Rude Q & A

What follows is a rude Q & A session that is based on questions I've received from Scrum Team members when they were introduced to Kanban. I hope it covers many of the questions you receive.

Q   Why are we evolving from Scrum by using Kanban?

A   The software industry continues to evolve. Kanban takes the benefits from Scrum a step further, enabling us to deliver improvements to our products and services and help us work continuously instead of depending on the artificial time boundaries of sprints.

Q   But time-boxing our sprints helps us stay focused and agile. Won't we lose that with Kanban?

A   Our focus comes from working on a limited number of items at once by time-boxing a sprint. Our agility comes from completing work and making it production-ready by the end of each sprint. Kanban directly limits the number of items we work on at once by limiting the number of work items in progress. Kanban ensures that every work item is production-ready the day it is completed, with clear done rules for each step of development. We keep our focus and agility but lose the artificial time boundaries. Now, every day is a day we can receive customer feedback. Every day is a day we can add value to our product. Every day is a day we can improve.

Q   But our sprint events forced us to get customer feedback. Won't we lose that with Kanban?

A   We need to engage customers constantly, and certainly not by imposing our timelines. It's true that Kanban alleviates the need for Sprint Planning, Sprint Review, and Sprint Retrospective events. But we still should be centering our decisions and designs on our customers' needs, preferences, and ambitions. Kanban enables us to do that anytime and all the time.

Q   But our Sprint Retrospectives encouraged us to improve. Won't we lose that with Kanban?

A   The Kanban board, work-in-progress (WIP) limits, and done rules make issues immediately apparent. There's no need to wait for the end of a sprint to fix the problems we're having with work-flow or quality. We shouldn't wait. We should fix problems with our product and our approach right away, and Kanban enables us to see the problems and resolve them as they happen. We also should be seeking improvements beyond the confines of our team and how we currently function. Continuous improvement is the hallmark of a great team, and we aspire to be great.

Q   Without the protection of a sprint, won't we get distracted by stakeholders outside the team?

A   Leadership, partners, customers, and others outside the team can provide feedback and influence the ordering of the backlog, but they can't interrupt work in progress any more than they can during sprints. The difference with Kanban is that new work from the backlog is taken up by the team continuously, which makes the team more responsive to stakeholders and their changing requirements.

Q   Without Sprint Planning, when do we break down features into tasks?

A   We'll break down features into releasable tasks during the specification step of our workflow. Our analysts will engage with customers and other team members to perform that step well, and they will also specify what the tasks should produce and achieve.

Q   Do those tasks need to be artificially tiny and uniform in size?

A   No, they only need to be similarly sized pieces of deliverable value (with each typically requiring one to five days to complete). We just want to avoid having large, poorly understood, and potentially unbounded work items clogging our workflow.

Q   Can we use photos of a whiteboard as specifications?

A   Absolutely. Specifications can range from detailed documents to whiteboard sketches—whatever best captures concisely and clearly what the tasks are that deliver the customer value that's desired.

Q   Aren't we all analysts? Doesn't everyone do everything in Kanban, like we do in Scrum?

A   All team members can do everything in Kanban, just like on Scrum Development Teams. In fact, Kanban has fewer specified roles than Scrum (no specific Product Owner or Scrum Master role). The analyst you assign to specify a feature can also implement or validate it, do both, or work on other features. With Kanban, you also can have specific people assigned to steps they excel at. The team decides how best to organize itself and can adapt as needed at any time.

Q   Then who is the Product Owner?

A   You can keep a single customer representative (Product Owner) if you want with Kanban, but you can also invite as many customers as you want to participate in product feedback and decision making. In particular, Chapter 3 describes how customers and other stakeholders can be involved in planning and ordering the backlog.

Q   If there's no Scrum Master, who unblocks tasks and engages the customer?

A   The signboard shows our work as cards that flow across the three product-development steps: Specify, Implement, and Validate. The WIP limits that set the right pacing are written above each step on the signboard, and the done rules are written below each step. Everyone will see when work is being blocked and bunched up. Because Kanban makes issues visible to everyone, everyone plays a part in unblocking tasks. Because the done rules ensure that the product is always production-ready, everyone can engage the customer.

Q   What about my Scrum Master training?

A   The techniques you learned as you trained to become a Scrum Master are as useful as ever. They'll help you work effectively across teams and with customers. You'll be better equipped to keep your team focused and productive. The difference with Kanban is that those responsibilities won't be yours alone—they are shared by your team.

Q   Without Sprint Planning, how do we avoid taking on too much work?

A   We set a pace that matches our team's sustainable throughput (delivery rate). That pace is synchronized across the three product-development steps by setting work-in-progress (WIP) limits for specification, implementation, and validation that make their throughput match our sustainable pace (details in the Kanban quick-start guide in Chapter 2). Naturally, our pace can change over time as work and staffing change. We can adjust our WIP limits at any time to maintain smooth workflow and the continuous delivery of customer value.

Q   Won't limiting work make us slower?

A   We're not limiting people, we're limiting the kinds of work they do. If implementation is stuck on a feature, specifying more features doesn't help. Instead, the team should work to unblock implementation (for example, clarify the spec, escalate an issue, research a customer preference, or bring in partner expertise). By focusing on keeping the work flowing smoothly and limiting work so that it maintains a smooth pace, we actually get more work done in less time.

Q Why not just move on to the next task?

A The key is the status of the blocked implementation task:

- If the task is blocked by an external dependency, we should move on to the next task until the old task is unblocked. We'll keep an eye on that blocked task in a special column on the signboard.

- If the task is blocked by a design question or issue, we need to unblock the task, ideally while the issue is still fresh in people's minds. The limits on work and the visibility of blocked tasks prevent us from ignoring design issues and letting them fester.

The same applies for blocked specification and validation tasks. Instead of letting problems pile up, we're going to work together to fix them quickly. That keeps work flowing smoothly, fixes issues before they permeate the product and become harder to repair, and delivers value faster and more continuously to our customers.

Q Where will the cards come from?

A We'll take our current Product Backlog, write the items on cards (if we haven't already), and place them in order on the left side of the signboard, in front of the specification step. When new work arrives or plans change, we'll add and rearrange the cards as needed.

Q Can we still do spikes?

A Absolutely. We control the backlog and the work. If we need a spike, we'll write it out on one or more cards, order them appropriately against the current backlog (usually at the top), and work on the spike together. We can time-box the spike by limiting the number of task cards. When the spike is complete, regular work will continue as usual from the top of the backlog.

Q When a card moves from one step to the next, who works on it?

A We'll assign work to whichever team member is free and capable of doing that work at the time (a practice followed by many Scrum Teams).

Q We already have a board that tracks progress. Have we been doing Kanban?

A Many Scrum Teams meet daily in front of a board that tracks their work progress. However, it's not Kanban unless you list your steps on the board (like Specify, Implement, and Validate), and each step has a work-in-progress (WIP) limit, a Done column, and a done rule clearly marked on the board.

Q Why does each step need its own Done column?

A Say you just completed implementing an item (it passes the implementation done rule). Without an implementation-specific check mark or implementation Done column, how would you indicate that the item is ready for validation? On an ordinary board, you just move the item to the validation step. However, that means the item is actively being validated and counts toward the validation WIP limit—neither of which is true. What's worse is that the item no longer counts toward the implementation WIP limit, so you're free to implement another item, even if validation is overwhelmed and needs help. The Done column for each step clearly indicates the status of each item and controls the flow of items in conjunction with their WIP limits.

Q   Who determines the done rules?

A   Our team decides on the done rules we'll follow. We know what causes issues. We know how to do our job well. We get to decide when a task should be considered done. Once we decide on the rules, we'll write them at the bottom of the signboard so that there's no confusion. Any time the rules need adjustment, we can change them together.

Q   Can we use test-driven development and pair programming with Kanban?

A   Certainly. We can leave the particular approach up to individual members or codify that all team members work a certain way by specifying the approach in our done rules. The important thing is for us to agree on our practices and rules. I discuss more about using various methods beyond Kanban and Scrum in Chapter 9, "Further resources and beyond."

Q   Does anything else change using Kanban?

A   Nope—that's it until we want to improve even further. For now, we'll have our daily standup in front of a signboard with our work steps written on it, cards showing our work, limits on the number of cards at each step, and rules at the bottom of the signboard that determine when a card is done with its current step. Whenever you're done with a step, based on the done rules, you'll move your card on the signboard and grab the next available card. If no cards are available, that indicates that workflow is blocked, and you should work with your teammates to unblock the flow.

Q   This actually sounds less complicated than Scrum. Why does Kanban work better?

A   With Scrum, we control the amount of unfinished work (work in progress) by time-boxing our work periods (our sprints). This helps us be agile and quickly deliver value and adjust our plans as requirements change. However, careful time-boxing requires extra planning and doesn't always account well for the variability of our work. Kanban directly limits the work in progress of broken-down tasks. This eliminates the need for extra planning and makes the workflow smooth. Issues are immediately apparent, so they don't fester and add excessive costs. Basically, Kanban does at a more direct level what Scrum was trying to do, which makes it simpler and more effective.

Checklist

Here's a checklist of actions for your team members to evolve from Scrum:

- ❏ Explain why evolving from Scrum is beneficial.

- ❏ Reassure team members that the adjustments should seem like refinements.

- ❏ As needed, decide as a team whether you'd like to divide the duties of Scrum Master and Product Owner among more people.

- ❏ Describe how Sprint Planning, Daily Scrum, Sprint Review, and Sprint Retrospective events evolve using Kanban.

- ❏ Perform the actions listed in the checklist in Chapter 2, "Kanban quick-start guide."

- ❏ Measure completed tasks and unresolved bugs, or whatever productivity and quality metrics you choose, on a regular basis.

- ❏ Celebrate productivity and quality improvement (as well as continuous delivery of value to customers).

- ❏ Answer any questions Scrum Team members have with respect and appreciation for all the progress they've made with Scrum and their continued improvement using Kanban.

CHAPTER 6

Deploying components, apps, and services

Chapter 3, "Hitting deadlines," describes how to fill the backlog on the left side of the Kanban board. This chapter covers how to deploy finished work from the right side of the signboard. Just as a well-organized and ordered backlog generates a smooth workflow through the steps on your signboard, your approach to deployment affects the continuous delivery of value to your customers.

Four common models are used to deploy a feature team's completed work:

- Integrate code from a development branch into the main line. This model is commonly used for large projects with centralized version control (and for many other kinds of projects).

- Submit a pull request or push code into a repository (often stored on a host such as GitHub). This model is commonly used for open source software (OSS) and distributed projects.

- Publish code, apps, or content to an online catalog or store (such as Google Play). This model is typically used for apps, software updates, and digital media.

- Propagate code and components to web servers or virtual machines. This model is typically used for websites, web services, and software as a service (SaaS).

For each of these models, I cover how to assign completed items to deployments, how to track when those items are deployed, and how the Kanban approach affects your deployment cadence and customer feedback mechanisms.

The topics covered are:
Continuous integration
Continuous push
Continuous publishing
Continuous deployment
Checklist

Continuous integration

Continuous integration is a software engineering practice that dates back to the early 1990s. This approach involves automating your build and testing it to the extent that you can integrate high-quality code changes with confidence into the main branch every day, perhaps even several times a day.

Kanban is a natural fit for continuous integration because the tasks you complete daily are production-ready; they certainly pass the criteria for integration. If you're working on a relatively small project that allows you to integrate into the main branch at will, your team can simply add this integration step as the last done rule for validation—no special tracking is necessary.

If you're on a large project with multiple branches and teams, integration into the main branch may be controlled, and for good reason. Integrations by different teams might have merge conflicts or interface conflicts (including call-signature, schema, and protocol conflicts). You need to control integrations into the main branch to manage the scope and breadth of the conflicts.

A mitigation strategy for managing integration conflicts is illustrated here:

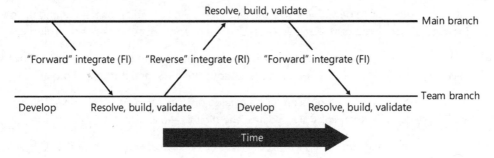

- Forward integrate from the main branch into your branch.

- Resolve any merge conflicts.

- Build the merged code.

- Validate the new build in case any interface (call-signature, schema, or protocol) conflicts occurred.

- Reverse integrate your merged changes back into the main branch.

This strategy fails if another team reverse integrates its changes while you are still validating yours. Timing issues such as this are common for projects with hundreds of engineers.

Large projects mitigate against timing issues by scheduling reverse integrations from different branches so that they do not overlap. A common approach is to do the following regularly (at least daily):

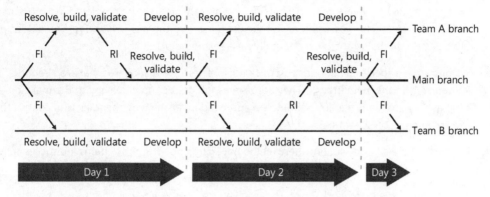

- Forward integrate from the main branch into all the child branches.

- Resolve any merge conflicts, build the child branches, and validate the builds.

- Reverse integrate the child branches on the basis of the times they are scheduled and their validation results.

- Resolve any merge conflicts, build the main branch, and validate the build.

> **Note** An alternative mitigation for integration conflicts is to divide your product into components with clear code boundaries and insist that changes to particular components happen only in assigned branches. This approach avoids merge conflicts between branches and allows multiple branches to be reverse integrated simultaneously. (You may still encounter interface conflicts at component boundaries, which can be mitigated by versioning interfaces.) Unfortunately, folks often ignore the branch rules, so this mitigation breaks down with centralized version control. However, it is a successful approach with distributed version control, as discussed in the "Continuous push" section later in this chapter.

If your project is following an integration schedule, the items in the rightmost column of your Kanban board may be done, but they aren't deployed to partner teams and customers until a reverse integration into the main branch. My teams divide the rightmost Done column into sections to track reverse integrations.

Backlog		Specify		Implement		Validate		
		(2)		(5)		(3)	Branch A	Deployed
□	□	□	□□□	□	□	□	□	□□□
□	□			□	□	□	Branch B	□□□
□	□			□		□	□	□□□
	□						FastTrack	□□□
							□	□□

- We use a section for every branch we work in. When a work item is completed, we move its note card to the section associated with the branch where the work was done. The note card stays there until that branch is successfully reverse integrated.

- We also have a special section for FastTrack items. These are work items that are needed immediately in the main branch. They are reverse integrated individually into the main line as soon as they are ready. FastTrack items are approved in advance by the folks who control the reverse integration schedule.

- Finally, we have a large section where all the note cards go after those items are successfully reserve integrated into the main branch.

You need to do a little extra work to track reverse integrations as you continuously integrate, but using simple sections on the right end of your signboard enables you to answer the question that all your partners and customers have: "Where are our requests?"

Inside Xbox

During the initial development phases of Xbox One, we had a fairly flat branch structure for the Xbox One platform. (Xbox Live services, SmartGlass, and apps such as TV and Party were coordinated separately.)

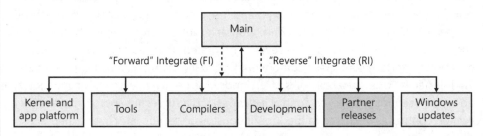

The Xbox One platform had a main branch and several child branches. Each child branch had a different focus: one for disruptive changes to the kernel and app platform, two for disruptive changes to the build system (tooling and compilers), one for day-to-day development, one for releases to partner teams, and one for Windows updates (the Xbox One platform is based on Windows). We'd run a reverse integration on the day-to-day branch a few times a week, when it was in good health, and the other branches as needed.

Once we started shipping platform releases to preview audiences and game developers once a month, we changed the platform branch structure to the one we use currently. In the following example, the current month is September.

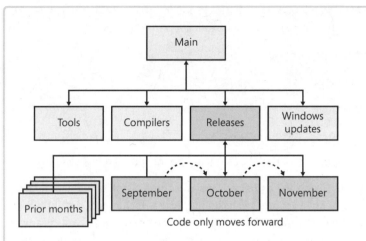

Code only moves forward

We moved nearly all development to monthly release branches, which we created under a Releases branch off Main. Fixes for the current month's release are made in the September branch. Day-to-day work scheduled to be released the next month occurs in the October branch. Work that won't make the October release happens in the November branch. Disruptive changes to tools and compilers still happen in branches under Main to isolate them from the more stable release branches. This allows stable code to be moved between monthly release branches, although that movement only goes forward, leaving past releases pristine in case we need to patch them later. We create the December branch when feature work is done on the October branch. This creates a continuous cycle of monthly releases with simple code movement.

Continuous push

Continuous push is continuous integration applied to distributed version control. Distributed version control systems, such as Git, allow teams and individuals to work independently in their own local, downstream clones of the upstream version control repository (a repo). When individuals or teams want to share their progress with one another, they push their changes from one repo to another—or, more politely, they request that the receiving person or team pull changes from one repo to another.

The upstream repo is often stored on a hosting service, such as GitHub. The owners of the upstream repo accept pull requests from the downstream repos used by contributing individuals and teams, validate the changes, and accept none, some, or all of the changes, depending on the validation results. For large projects, multiple repos may be stored on the hosting service, with one or more related components in each repo.

As with continuous integration, Kanban is a natural fit for continuous push because the tasks you complete daily are production-ready—they certainly pass the criteria that makes them prime for pushing to the upstream repo (or for submitting through a pull request). And as in continuous integration, large projects need to mitigate against merge and interface conflicts when new code is pushed to the upstream repo. The mitigation follows a familiar pattern:

- Pull from the upstream repo into your repo.

- Resolve any merge conflicts.

- Build the merged code.

- Validate the new build against interface conflicts.

- Push your merged changes back into the upstream repo (or submit a pull request).

A timing issue is involved, just like with centralized version control. Conflict mitigation fails if another repo pushes its changes while you are still validating yours. Fortunately, distributed version control allows the owners of the upstream repo to control the flow of changes. Owners can choose the order of the pull requests they take and can validate each one in separate branches within personal repositories or the upstream repo. Thus, the team submitting the pull request may want to track when its request is accepted and complete.

You can track your pull requests by dividing the rightmost Done column of your signboard into sections for each repo.

Backlog		Specify		Implement			Validate	
		(2)		(5)		(3)	Repo A ┊ Deployed	
☐	☐	☐	☐☐☐	☐	☐	☐	☐☐ ┊ ☐☐☐	
☐	☐			☐	☐	☐	Repo B ┊ ☐☐☐	
☐	☐			☐		☐	☐☐☐ ┊ ☐☐☐	
	☐						FastTrack ┊ ☐☐☐	
							☐ ┊ ☐☐	

- Include a section for each repo you work in. When a work item is completed, move its note card to the section associated with the repo where the work was done. The note card stays there until the pull request is accepted and complete.

- Add a special section for FastTrack items. These are work items that are needed immediately in the upstream repo. They get pulled individually into the upstream repo as soon as they are ready. FastTrack items are requested in advance by the owners of the upstream repo.

- Finally, include a large section where all the note cards go after they have successfully been pulled into the upstream repo.

A little extra work is needed to track pull requests, but using simple sections on the right end of your signboard enables you to answer the question that all your partners and customers have: "When will our requests be available?"

Inside Xbox

Xbox Live services and most inbox Xbox One apps (such as TV and Party) are developed separately from the Xbox One platform code. Their source is stored in Visual Studio Team Foundation Server (TFS). Each service and app team stores and builds its source separately and works fairly independently. Some teams prefer to use Git for version control and some prefer TFS Version Control (a centralized version control system in TFS). The teams using Git store their upstream repo in the TFS Git system.

The inbox apps such as TV and Party, which come preinstalled on Xbox One systems, must be packaged with the operating system when we do system updates. Because we publish updates every day, the packaging of inbox apps happens with the nightly build. However, the apps and platform are independently changed and built. This creates a synchronization problem.

We solve the synchronization problem by referencing daily builds of the platform SDK on the app build machines each morning. Apps are built and then tested against the new SDK throughout the day. Before the next night's packaging commences, we sync the most recently built apps to the platform packaging machines. This could still make the apps off by a single day if someone changed the platform SDK app interfaces that day.

To resolve the off-by-a-day issue, we check for app interface changes during rolling platform builds throughout the day. When one is detected, the results from the rolling platform build are used to patch the SDK referenced by the app build machines. This step is admittedly convoluted. Ideally, apps would install independently of the platform, and the SDK would have versioned interfaces, even for inbox apps. But at Xbox, we like to move fast and make changes every day, so we needed a compromise to achieve continuous delivery while still giving app teams the freedom to develop independently.

Continuous publishing

Continuous publishing started in the early 2000s as content providers moved online and realized that many publications (user guides, record albums, newspapers, journals, magazines, and reference books) were no longer immutable formats. The concepts of story deadlines and final copies of manuals were replaced by publishing content as soon as it was ready, and updating it based on changing circumstances and customer feedback. Other forms of content, such as videos, apps, and software updates, also moved to a continuous publishing model as they became available for digital download or streaming.

Kanban is a natural fit for continuous publishing because the tasks you complete daily are production-quality, and thus ready for publication. If you are publishing to your own online catalog or store, your team can simply add publishing as the last done rule for validation—no special tracking is necessary.

When publishing software changes (apps and updates), many content providers restrict the initial audience to a preview or beta group. That way, if unusual or uncaught issues arise, the impact is minimized. Once the preview or beta group has consumed the new content without issues, the audience can be expanded. This approach to restricting audiences can also be used to reward preferred customers with premier content.

If you are publishing your app or update to a third-party catalog or store—like Google Play, the Microsoft Store, or iTunes—the publishing process may be long and arduous, requiring you to batch up completed work and publish only weekly or monthly. As a result, the items in the rightmost column of your Kanban board may be done, but they aren't deployed to customers until the latest app or update submission is successfully published. You can track your pending submissions by dividing the rightmost Done column of your signboard into sections.

Backlog		Specify (2)		Implement (5)		Validate (3)	Pending	Deployed
☐	☐	☐	☐☐☐	☐	☐	☐	☐☐	☐☐☐
☐	☐			☐	☐	☐	☐	☐☐☐
☐	☐			☐		☐	Submitted	☐☐☐
	☐						☐☐☐	☐☐☐
							☐	☐☐

- When a work item is completed, move its note card to the Pending section. The note card stays there until the next app or update is submitted. There's no WIP limit because the Pending section is part of the last Done column, though having an unusually large number of items there might indicate a submission problem.

- When an app or update is submitted, move all the pending note cards to the Submitted section.

- Finally, when the app or update submission is published, move the note cards to the large Deployed section.

Tracking submissions requires you to do a little extra work, but using simple sections on the right end of your signboard enables you to answer the question that all your stakeholders and customers have: "When will our requests be published and available?"

Inside Xbox

Xbox does a great deal of continuous publishing. As I mentioned in previous sections (and detailed in Chapter 4, "Adapting from Waterfall"), we publish platform and inbox app updates daily to a variety of preview audiences: internal "dog food" users, internal early adopters, and public preview groups. We publish those updates worldwide each month. Each day we also publish editorial content worldwide to the Xbox One home screen, the Xbox.com website, and Xbox Music and Video. Naturally, we also continuously publish other game and app updates, as well as additional downloadable content for those games and apps.

The systems we use for continuous publishing vary by content type. App, game, and platform updates go through the game-ingestion pipeline. Music and videos go through encoding pipelines before having their metadata indexed by Bing. Editorial content for the Xbox One home screen, the Xbox.com website, and Xbox Music and Video features is published by our content-management system.

Our individual publishing systems share certain attributes:

- They can publish content on demand or on a special schedule (such as being timed to a particular release date).

- They can control the audience for any piece of content. This is particularly important for handling differing licensing and standards of appropriate content in different locales for different age groups. It also helps manage preview and premier content.

- They can manage content in multiple languages targeting multiple devices. We often publish portions of the same editorial content for the Xbox One home screen, Xbox.com, and SmartGlass on Windows PCs, Surface, Windows Phone, Android devices, and the iPad and iPhone.

- With so much continuous publishing, it's handy to have a simple system such as Kanban to track what work is being published to what targets and when. We also use tools like Visual Studio Team Foundation Server (TFS) and the publishing systems directly to track our work, depending on each team's preference.

Continuous deployment

Continuous deployment started in the mid-2000s as web companies realized significant gains in productivity and customer feedback by automatically deploying main-line builds directly to production. Deploying a build directly to production after automated testing may strike longtime software engineers and managers as a risky proposition. However, in practice, continuous deployment has few risks and many advantages over extensively testing builds in preproduction environments before deploying to production.

- Like continuous publishing, continuous deployment makes use of audience control. A new build in production is initially exposed to a very limited audience (perhaps as small as just the feature team). Assuming the build functions properly, the audience is expanded in stages from a larger internal group, to a limited external group, to the broader public, and finally to the full public.

- Continuous deployment relies on monitoring and instrumentation to recognize when new builds are faulty, consume too many resources, or both. Without monitoring, you wouldn't notice problems until they were serious enough to affect customers. Without instrumentation, you couldn't pinpoint the issues with a build and resolve them. There are frameworks, such as Microsoft Azure's Application Insights, that can help you achieve the monitoring and instrumentation you need.

- Naturally, continuous deployment depends on an automated system to deploy builds. In case an issue comes up, the deployment system must also be capable of an automated rollback (switching back to a previous good build). Fortunately, modern cloud computing providers such as Amazon Web Services (AWS) and Microsoft Azure provide these automated systems.

- With audience control, monitoring, instrumentation, and automated deployment and roll-backs in place, you no longer need preproduction environments. Those environments are costly to build and maintain, and they rarely function quite like production environments because of differences in scale, load, networking, hardware, customer data, business data, and configuration settings. Instead, you test in production.

- By testing in production, you gain greater assurance that your builds will function properly in the real production environment, you save the time spent in preproduction (since you have to test in production anyway), and you gain valuable early customer feedback (including A/B testing and other experimentation).

Areas of your service that are too risky to deploy to production without extensive testing, such as the handling of personally identifiable information (PII) and monetary transactions, still need to go through preproduction environments. However, those areas are a small subset of overall service functionality, even for a site like Amazon.com. (Amazon was an early adopter of continuous deployment.)

Note What I refer to as continuous deployment is sometimes called "continuous delivery." Those who call it continuous delivery differentiate between deploying to production only the builds that the team chooses ("continuous delivery") and automatically deploying every build to production ("continuous deployment"). It is important to be clear about which approach your team decides to take.

Kanban is a natural fit for continuous deployment because the tasks you complete daily are production-quality, and thus ready for deployment. If you are deploying to your own independently versioned web service or site, your team can simply add deployment as the last done rule for validation—no special tracking is necessary.

If your team's efforts are part of a large collection of tightly integrated services, you might need to batch up completed work and deploy only weekly or monthly (except for quick fixes that get deployed daily). As a result, the items in the rightmost column of your Kanban board may be done, but they aren't available to customers until the next integrated service deployment. You can track your pending deployments by dividing the rightmost Done column of your signboard into sections.

Backlog		Specify		Implement		Validate		
		(2)		(5)		(3)	Pending	Deployed
☐	☐	☐	☐☐☐	☐	☐	☐	☐☐☐	☐☐☐
☐	☐			☐	☐	☐	☐☐☐	☐☐☐
☐	☐			☐		☐	☐☐	☐☐☐
	☐						Quick fix	☐☐☐
							☐	☐☐

- When a work item is completed, move its note card to the Pending section. The note card stays there until the next integrated service deployment. There's no WIP limit because the Pending section is part of the last Done column, though having an unusually large number of items there might indicate a deployment problem.

- There's a special section for quick-fix items. These work items are usually fixes to issues that are serious enough to fix within a day or two but not serious enough to require a rollback of an entire deployment.

- Once items are deployed to production, move their note cards to the large Deployed section.

You need to do a little extra work to track deployments, but using simple sections on the right end of your signboard enables you to answer the question that all your stakeholders and customers have: "When will our requests be live in production?"

Inside Xbox

When I first joined the Xbox division in 2010, Xbox had eight service environments: development, check-in testing, scenario testing, stress testing, cross-division integration, partner integration, certification, and production. Using all those environments, we deployed to production every few months, with a goal to deploy every six weeks.

My teams at the time were responsible for all the Microsoft gaming websites, including Xbox.com. We worked closely with the Xbox Live social services group. Our two groups of teams had many deployment issues and started tackling them one at a time. First, we got continuous integration working, then automated deployment and rollback, then monitoring and instrumentation, then audience control, and finally continuous deployment. The changes were difficult, but in less than two years we were deploying every two weeks with quick fixes as needed daily.

We weren't the only groups at Microsoft that adopted continuous deployment. Bing and Ads adopted the approach before Xbox, and all of Xbox Live adopted it after that group's teams saw that continuous deployment clearly worked and its automation, customer feedback, monitoring, and testing in production were essential to running modern services at scale. Xbox now has only two service environments (integration and production), and deploys to production at will (several times a day).

New Xbox services today are built separately as independently versioned projects in Visual Studio Team Foundation Server (TFS). Our TFS build system automatically runs unit tests against each build, performs localization and signing as needed, and then deploys each build directly to its target environment based on the branch (there are development branches and production branches).

Because each modern service is a separate project, we never need to worry about merge conflicts across teams. However, interface conflicts are still possible. That's why we independently version each modern service and have multiple versions of each service deployed to production.

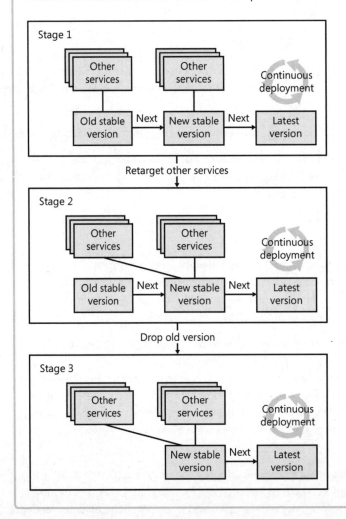

With instrumentation, each service team can tell which of its versions are being used by other service teams. They can then contact the other teams, let them know when old versions of the service are being deprecated, and smoothly transition the other services to a more recent stable version.

Meanwhile, they can carry on the continuous deployment of the latest version without worrying about interface conflicts.

Continuous deployment of our services is a beautiful system that supports our continuous publishing of the platform and apps and our continuous integration of value for customers.

Checklist

Here's a checklist of actions for deploying components, apps, and services by using Kanban:

- ❏ For continuous integration of changes:

    - Follow an integration strategy for your team branch that avoids merge and interface conflicts.

    - Divide the rightmost Done column of your signboard into sections for each branch you use and special sections for FastTrack changes and deployed changes.

    - Use the Done sections to track integrations of completed work.

- ❏ For continuous push of changes:

    - Follow a pull-and-push (or pull request) strategy for your team repo that avoids merge and interface conflicts.

    - Divide the rightmost Done column of your signboard into sections for each repo you use and special sections for FastTrack changes and deployed changes.

    - Use the Done sections to track pushes or pull requests of completed work.

- ❏ For continuous publishing of apps and content:

    - Divide the rightmost Done column of your signboard into Pending, Submitted, and Deployed sections.

    - Use the Done sections to track the publishing state of completed work.

- ❏ For continuous deployment of services:

    - Use a service deployment tool that provides audience control, automated deployment, and automated rollback.

    - Ensure that your service monitoring and instrumentation notices and pinpoints service issues before your customers are affected.

    - Test your services in production. If your services handle highly sensitive information, such as personally identifiable information (PII) and monetary transactions, you may want to test changes in a preproduction environment first.

- Divide the rightmost Done column of your signboard into Pending, Quick Fix, and Deployed sections.

- Use the Done sections to track the deployment state of completed work.

CHAPTER 7

Using Kanban within large organizations

If you work for a small IT group or on an independent app, game, service, or some other small independent project, this chapter is not for you. Your job is somewhat free from large-scale coordination, planning, alignment, tracking, and other mechanisms necessary to steer large projects with hundreds or thousands of participants. You still need to deal with budgets, fickle customers and management, and changing requirements from a variety of sources, but you can otherwise enjoy your independence and deliver continuous value with Kanban.

If you work on large projects within large organizations, you need mechanisms to guide, coordinate, and track the work of the vast number of people involved. However, this is not a book about high-level strategic planning, crowdsourcing, or classic project management—there are good books and materials available on those subjects. This book is about using Kanban effectively in a variety of situations, including within large organizations.

In a large organization, different teams often use different project-management methods. Your feature team (3–10 people) might use Kanban, carry little technical debt (bugs, shortcuts, and regrettable decisions), and always have production-ready code. Other feature teams might use traditional Waterfall, Scrummerfall (traditional Waterfall with short, fixed-length milestones called "Sprints"), Scrum, Extreme Programming (XP), or some other development approach. Those other teams may have different expectations about quality and whether their shared components are production-ready, depending on the stage of the project. This can make coordination across teams quite tricky. To be successful, your team needs to align its backlog of work to the larger project plan, order its work to meet the needs of dependent partner teams, fit its work within project milestones, communicate status to the larger project, handle when the components your team depends on are of poor quality or late, and stay busy when all your work is complete but your partner teams are stabilizing theirs. I provide recommendations for managing each of these areas in the following sections.

The topics covered are:
Deriving a backlog from big upfront planning
Ordering work based on dependencies
Fitting into milestones
Communicating status up and out
Dealing with late or unstable dependencies
Staying productive during stabilization
Checklist

Deriving a backlog from big upfront planning

When you are running a large project that involves hundreds or thousands of people, it's important to have a vision and a plan for achieving your project goals. Even crowdsourcing projects need an organizing principle and structure to allow everyone to contribute toward the shared outcome. The high-level plan and structure of large projects usually take a few forms:

- A high-level vision for what the end product will be. This may include a visualization, a list of capabilities and any constraints, a set of targeted customer segments and supported scenarios, and even an anticipated press release for when the project is complete.

- A high-level architecture that lays out how components and contributions to the product fit and work together to achieve the product vision.

- A high-level schedule for product development with milestones for the key events (like conferences, press announcements, or launch), key dates when major product capabilities come together, and expected dates when target metrics (such as performance, scale, or participation) are reached. (Here, "milestone" means a key date, not necessarily a traditional Waterfall milestone.)

Creating a high-level vision, architecture, and schedule prior to starting a large project is essential to success, but it can be overdone. Too much big upfront planning tends to be wasteful, since there are many unknowns and requirements often change. Unfortunately, too little planning can lead to chaos and failure, even if some feature teams succeed in building their individual parts. In my experience, you want just enough planning to organize the project and coordinate all the people involved, knowing that the high-level vision, architecture, and schedule will change as the project progresses. However, this chapter isn't about creating large project plans (there are many other books on that topic); it's about using Kanban within that edifice.

After the initial high-level plan is in place, individual teams need to know how they contribute to the vision, how their contribution fits into the architecture, and how their work aligns to the schedule. That knowledge is used to derive and order each team's backlog. Let's start with the vision and architecture.

Two common approaches, shown in Figure 7-1, are used for how individual teams contribute to a vision and fit into an architecture:

- **By scenario** Each individual team owns a different scenario described in the vision (such as, "Taking a photo and sharing it with friends"). The team creates the components laid out in the architecture as needed for its scenario. Those components are refactored and augmented as needed by other teams for their scenarios. The scenario approach ensures complete end-to-end experiences, but it may result in poorly engineered components constructed by too many hands. A team's backlog is derived by breaking down the team's assigned scenario into individual features or stories.

- **By component** Each individual team owns a component laid out in the architecture (such as the photo-manipulation library). The component teams that own the UI typically stitch together scenarios described in the vision using lower-level components. This component approach provides clear boundaries for teams, and well-structured components, but it may result in unwieldy or incomplete end-to-end experiences. A team's backlog is derived by breaking down the team's assigned component into individual features or requirements.

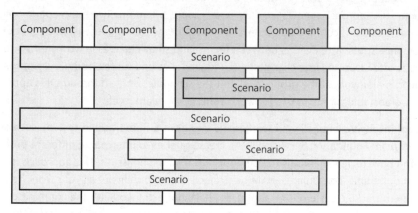

FIGURE 7-1 Components with scenarios that cut across them.

Tip Personally, I've had the most success with a hybrid approach (shown in dark gray in Figure 7-1). You assign each feature team of 3–10 members a set of related components as well as ownership of smaller scenarios that work primarily within those components. Each team creates its components as it constructs its scenarios and also collaborates on the larger end-to-end scenarios. The end-to-end scenarios tend to fit together better as a result of the work on the smaller scenarios. Each team's backlog is derived by breaking down its components and scenarios into features, stories, and requirements.

Ordering work based on dependencies

In Chapter 3, "Hitting deadlines," I describe how to populate your backlog, establish your minimum viable product (MVP), order work (including technical debt), estimate features and tasks, track the expected completion date, and right-size your team. The only differences within a large project are the following:

- Your team's MVP is constrained by the boundaries of the overall MVP and the scenarios and components that your team owns. Your team should step outside those boundaries only with the agreement of leadership and your partner teams. Otherwise, be prepared to face the wrath of your leadership and partners when they discover that you perverted their planning.

- Your ordering of work is heavily influenced by the partner teams that depend on you and the partner teams you depend on. That's the focus of this section.

There are many ways to coordinate the order of your team's work with the work of other teams. Here are a few common approaches:

- **Automatic** Put all the teams' work items into a project-management system (such as Microsoft Project or LiquidPlanner), indicate dependencies, and let the system order work items for you. This approach seems fast, easy, and reliable, but in practice the preparation is time-consuming and difficult, the schedule is only as good as your manual list of dependencies, you can miss subtle interactions between teams, and small changes in work items and dependencies often lead to large changes in scheduling. I've had success using this approach for scheduling major work at the group level, but the schedules derived through this approach have been too unstable for me to use for work items at the team level.

- **Manual, tool intensive** Put all your work items into a work-item tracking system (such as Visual Studio Team Foundation Server or JIRA), create queries to interrogate different product areas, and have review meetings to work out potential timing issues. This approach is effective but quite time-consuming. For large projects, you typically put all your work items into a work-item tracking system for tracking, so that's not extra work. It's the combinatorics of cross-team dependencies that lead to weeks of cross-team review meetings. You often need to meet with teams two or three times, for an hour or more each time. Once the ordering is set, most teams keep meeting weekly, like a Scrum of Scrums, to make regular adjustments based on progress.

- **Manual, socially intensive** Have all your teams meet as a large group, place all your work items for the next six months in order on a long wall (each row representing a different team, each wide column a different month), walk along the wall noting timing issues (dependencies out of order and too much work in a month), have 15-minute meetings in pairs of teams to discuss the issues (teams sign up to meet), reorder items on the wall, walk along the wall again, and repeat these steps until every team feels good about the order. This is my favorite approach because it creates a visualization of upcoming work and has a short duration (a single day or an afternoon). However, it works only for 10 or fewer teams at a time, and you must repeat these big meetings every three to four months.

These methods can be used in combination at different levels of scale. If you've got a project with teams of 8 members, who work for groups of 8 teams, who are part of divisions of 8 groups, who work within an organization with 16 divisions, that's more than 8,000 people on the project. For this example, shown in Figure 7-2, each level of scale might use a different method:

- To coordinate divisions within an organization, you could use the automatic or tool-intensive approach with group managers, division heads, and the organization leader. The work items would be at the highest level (end-to-end scenarios and major components), but they would provide to leadership the guidance needed to set expectations for their divisions, customers, and partners and lay out a milestone road map for the project.

- To coordinate groups within a division, you could use the automatic, tool-intensive, or socially intensive approach with team leads, group managers, and the division head. The work items would be at a high level (scenarios and key component areas), but they would serve to organize the groups and clarify priorities and ordering for the teams.

- To coordinate teams within a group, I'd recommend using the socially intensive approach with all the people on the eight teams, their leads, and the group manager. That achieves the ordering of work items in a single day and allows for replanning every few months. (I've seen many groups use the tool-intensive approach effectively to coordinate teams, including my own, but it takes much longer and still misses issues.)

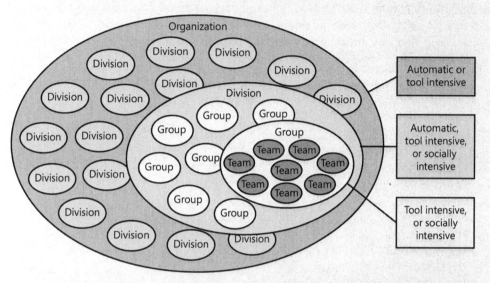

FIGURE 7-2 Coordination approaches at different levels of organization hierarchy.

I've been on projects with more than 8,000 people. Different scheduling approaches are commonly used at different levels. While some purists yearn for one system that can schedule work across every level of scale, in practice that doesn't appear to be necessary or even appropriate (different scales really are different). However, having one system for tracking does prove useful. I talk about that in the "Communicating status up and out" section. I touch on related questions in the section "Dealing with late or unstable dependencies" later in this chapter.

Inside Xbox

Large project planning at Microsoft typically starts bottom up and finishes top down. Each small team lists the work they'd like to do. Those lists get collected at the group level and then reviewed at the division and organization levels. At the same time, market research, product planning, business planning, and design collect the high-level work they'd like feature teams to do. All this input is fashioned into a product vision, architecture, and schedule. The schedule is then adjusted for dependencies and other considerations as it is pushed back down through the divisions, groups, and teams. In the end, each team has an ordered list of work.

Large project planning often takes a few months to complete, and thus it is used only for long-term planning and massive projects, like Windows 10 or the initial launch of Xbox One. When Microsoft shipped packaged products once every few years, the few months of planning were also used to give people needed vacations and to work on prototypes, analyze product issues, improve infrastructure, and reduce various forms of technical debt. These days in Xbox, long-term planning happens in parallel with our continuous publishing and deployment.

My Xbox.com teams used the socially intensive approach and got quite good at it. We could replan in just a few hours each quarter. My current teams use a combination of McGrath and MacMillan's Options Portfolio for strategic planning (see Figure 7-3) and dynamic ordering of our Kanban backlog based on customer requests and usage data.

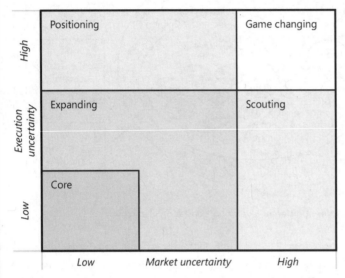

FIGURE 7-3 The basic grid used for planning with the McGrath and MacMillan Options Portfolio.

McGrath and MacMillan's Options Portfolio has you place your current and future work focus on a two-dimensional grid. The higher you are on the vertical axis, the more execution risk is involved (technical or operational). The farther right you are on the horizontal axis, the more market risk is involved (customer or competitive). The lower-left corner tends to hold your current core capabilities. The upper right holds game-changing ideas. For strategic planning, you want a balanced portfolio, with work spread across all portions of the grid—not enough in the core and your current business suffers; not enough on the edges and you've got no future business. Each year, my teams spend 5–10 hours, spread over a couple of weeks, to bring together all the customer feedback and technical ideas they've had, fill out their portfolios, and review them with me. We've found it to be a fast, simple, and flexible framework that provides insight, motivation, and results.

Fitting into milestones

After your team's backlog is populated and ordered, you can start continuously delivering value to your customers and partner teams using Kanban. However, your leadership and partner teams may want to know what work items will be available at each project milestone. If you don't need to provide this information, you can skip this section and the estimation work involved because what really matters is prioritization (covered in "Ordering work based on dependencies") and knowing when work is actually delivered (covered in "Communicating status up and out").

If you are required to fit delivery of work items into project milestones, follow the procedure I outline in the section "Track expected completion date" in Chapter 3 for each work item. It looks like this:

- Compute your team's task add rate (TAR) and task completion rate (TCR).

- Estimate the number of tasks comprising each work item.

- For each work item, sum the current task estimates (CTE) for the item and all its predecessors.

- Divide that CTE sum by TCR minus TAR to get the estimated number of days until each work item is complete.

- Fit your work items into project milestones based on their completion dates.

- If you want to be conservative, include only work items that are estimated to be completed a couple of weeks prior to their milestone target.

Figure 7-4 shows a worksheet that computes the estimated completion dates for you. (You can download an Excel file with the formulas.)

	A	B	C	D	E
1	Fitting into milestones		Fill in cells with yellow highlight		
2					
3	Task add rate (TAR)	Task completion rate (TCR)	Start date		
4	0.10	0.76	11/3/2014		
5					
6	Work item	Task estimate (TE)	Current task estimate (CTE = Sum of TE)	Days till complete (CTE / (TCR – TAR))	Expected completion date
7	[Work item 1]	4	4	6	11/9/2014
8	[Work item 2]	6	10	15	11/18/2014
9	[Work item 3]	2	12	18	11/21/2014
10	[Work item 4]	5	17	26	11/28/2014
11	[Work item 5]	4	21	32	12/4/2014
12	[Work item 6]	1	22	33	12/6/2014
13	[Work item 7]	3	25	38	12/10/2014
14	[Work item 8]	3	28	42	12/15/2014
15	[Work item 9]	5	33	50	12/23/2014
16	[Work item 10]	4	37	56	12/29/2014

FIGURE 7-4 Calculation of expected completion date for an ordered set of work items.

In this example, 10 work items vary in estimated size from 1 to 6 tasks. They represent the deliverables expected of your team in the order you've established with the organization. Their task estimates are summed to compute the current task estimate (CTE), which is then divided by TCR minus

TAR to find the days until that work item and all its predecessors will be complete. That count of days is then added to the start date to determine the expected completion date. Please note that this simple date computation assumes weekends are included in the TAR and TCR calculations.

> **Tip** These date estimates can also be used for scheduling discussions. For example, the socially intensive approach to ordering your backlog calls for placing work items in month columns. You can place work items based on your gut experience or use these date estimates as an initial cut. For estimated start dates, simply use the completion date of the previous item (rough, but close enough for scheduling purposes). Please keep in mind that all estimates are subject to the replanning inherent in any complex project with changing requirements.

Communicating status up and out

To customers, your management, and your partner teams, when you complete a work item is more important than your estimate of that date. They are interested in the status of your work items to see overall progress, to take note of any unexpected delays, to help where they can, and to update plans if any items come in particularly early or late.

Large organizations typically track project status using an online work-item tracking system, such as Visual Studio Team Foundation Server or JIRA, or an online project-management system, such as Microsoft Project Server or LiquidPlanner. Because your team tracks work items continuously on your Kanban board, no extra effort is needed to collect status information. Once a day, one of your team members just synchronizes the items on your signboard with the items in your project's online tracking system (perhaps at the beginning or end of each day or before or after the daily standup). Doing this is straightforward and takes only a few minutes.

Some online tracking systems can also display work items in a virtual signboard view. While online tracking systems are often essential for large projects, virtual signboards aren't as necessary and might introduce problems. Before you switch to a virtual signboard, consider the following:

- **Does the virtual signboard display your backlog, plus an Active and Done column for each of your software development steps?** Some virtual signboards have only one Done column at the end, which causes items to move between steps prematurely and count against the wrong work-in-progress (WIP) limit, leading to persistent workflow issues. (Details in the rude Q & A sections in Chapters 4 and 5.)

- **Does the virtual signboard display your chosen WIP limits and done rules for each step?** The system doesn't need to enforce WIP limits or rules because your team should be the one in control, but it is nice if the system automatically highlights flow issues.

- **Is it fast and easy to create new items, reorder them in the backlog, and move them on the signboard?** These operations are common and should take only a few seconds (including time to engage the signboard). If they are cumbersome, team members will abandon their use of the signboard, defeating its purpose and sabotaging effective Kanban.

Other nice features include having separate swim lanes for different types of work items, tags to track the origin of work items and special status, and various date, priority, and estimation fields that assist in planning. I'd especially appreciate a simple supported workflow for breaking down work items into tasks, where the tasks are associated with each other and the original work item.

Perhaps we'll soon have wall-sized touch displays that are as easy to use and versatile as a physical signboard. Until that day, I don't recommend using a virtual signboard unless you have a physically distributed team.

For major deliverables and breaking changes to APIs, it's not enough to passively provide detailed status through your online tracking system. You need to actively announce major deliverables and breaking changes to customers, management, and partner teams.

Major deliverables are worth announcing proactively, not for vanity's sake (though you've earned a little celebration), but for notifying your customers, management, and partner teams that important new work can be utilized and validated broadly. If it really was a major deliverable, those people will be eagerly awaiting it and will assume it's late if you only passively mark its last work item complete.

Breaking changes are critical to announce, especially to customers and partner teams. These are changes to APIs, file formats, protocols, and other interfaces that break old usage patterns. Ideally, your team minimizes the impact of interface changes by updating client code and libraries, providing shims, or versioning interfaces so that only new use is affected. However, it's sometimes necessary to make breaking changes on interfaces under development. A formal announcement that is easily recognized and understood is essential to keep your customers and partners in your good graces.

While announcements of major deliverables and breaking changes are not special to Kanban, they are important to call out because Kanban changes your cadence. With traditional Waterfall or Scrum, teams often reach major deliverables and integrate breaking changes at milestone or sprint boundaries. With Kanban, those events happen continuously, so it's important to have good communication habits in place.

Inside Xbox

Xbox uses Visual Studio Team Foundation Server (TFS) as its online work-item tracking system for large projects. We use it for tracking customer promises, scenarios, features, stories, tasks, and bugs. It serves its purpose well and has a great interface with Excel, which is a boon to Excel geeks like me. TFS supports work-item hierarchies, which allows us to tie tasks to features and stories, which in turn are tied to scenarios and customer promises. Aside from the usual fields that cover assignment, priority, rank, area, status, title, description, history, and so on, we also track target release. Whereas other fields might capture when an item is done, a target release field captures when an item will reach customers.

We announce major deliverables via email to Xbox-wide distribution lists. It's always exciting to hear about major new functionality becoming available. Often, these announcements will come with detailed descriptions and even have a rude Q & A like the ones I provided at the end of Chapters 4 and 5 of this book. It's important for the organization to understand what is and is not included in each deliverable.

We use even broader distribution lists to communicate Xbox breaking changes. The messages about breaking changes follow a structured template that lists the name of the change, impact rating (low, medium, and high), summary, reason for change, and contacts. During the year leading up to the Xbox One launch, multiple breaking-change messages were sent each week. A year after the launch, the count is down to less than one a month.

Dealing with late or unstable dependencies

Even if you carefully coordinate the ordering of work with partner teams and regularly give and receive status, your workflow can still be dramatically affected by late or unstable dependencies. Late dependencies have a cascading effect on schedules, regardless of what product-development approach you use. I'll discuss strategies to deal with them effectively within Kanban.

Unstable dependencies are particularly troubling to Scrum and Kanban teams. In addition to delaying the completion of tasks (just as late dependencies do), unstable dependencies expose a cultural difference between teams that often leads to frustration, tension, and breakdowns in communication. I'll provide strategies to handle unstable dependencies constructively.

Late dependencies

When a scenario or component that your team depends on is late, that delays your scenario and component work, making your work late for teams further down the chain. If that dependency chain is part of the critical chain of the project (the chain of work items that constrains the length of the whole project), day-to-day slips by one team result in day-to-day slips for the entire project.

You can handle late dependencies effectively with Kanban in several ways:

- Place blocked items in a Track column in the Implement step as described in the "Trouble-shooting" section of the Kanban quick-start guide (Chapter 2). Each day, team members assigned to blocked items report on progress in unblocking the items. Once items are unblocked, the items resume implementation.

- Create a simple fake implementation of your dependency, similar to a mock object, but instead of using the object for unit testing, use it to unblock downstream implementation. The fake is intentionally incomplete and unsophisticated—it contains just enough functionality for you to validate your key scenarios and components and unblock the teams that depend on you.

When you create the fake, also create a new task for removing the fake, and put that task's note card in the Track column of the Implement step. As soon as your upstream partner team completes the real work, you can remove the fake and validate that everything still functions properly. Doing the extra work to create and later throw away a fake may be worth it only for items in the project's critical chain.

- Write a shim between a prior stable version of your dependency and the anticipated future version that's late. The shim is like a fake but is more functional because it's built on top of a working prior version. As with the fake, you need to create a new task for removing the shim and validate the full new version when your upstream partner team completes the real work.

- Assist your upstream partner team, perhaps even to the point of taking over the work on your dependency. Because you share the success and failure of the entire project with all your partner teams, helping them out on the highest-priority work should always be an option. However, taking on another team's work can be challenging politically and technically. It may also jeopardize the portion of your backlog that isn't affected by the late dependency. If the particular situation warrants getting involved, have a discussion with your partner team and help out where it makes sense.

Dealing with late dependencies can be frustrating and cause extra work, but that work is unavoidable. Being constructive and acting to avoid downstream impact helps everyone. Remember, one day the person causing the delay may be you.

Unstable dependencies

When an upstream dependency is unstable (incomplete, with many quality issues), that's the same for your team's purposes as the dependency being late. You can't specify, implement, and validate that your work is production-ready if the scenarios or components it depends on aren't production-ready themselves. However, even if your upstream partner team acknowledges that their work is unstable, they may still believe it is complete. This fundamental difference in viewpoint can cause frustration, tension, and misunderstandings.

Your upstream partner team might consider its unstable deliverables complete for several reasons:

- The partner team could simply be a poor-quality team as the result of inappropriate staffing, faulty practices, negligent leadership, or a mix of these factors. The team's members might be wonderful people, but their deliverables are unreliable.

- The team might be following a traditional Waterfall model, where specification, implementation, and validation happen in bulk. The team might consider an individual scenario, feature, story, or component complete as soon as it's implemented, but well before it is validated. Team members might use terms such as "code complete" or "feature complete" to describe their current work status. ("Test complete" and "release candidate" milestones may be months away.)

- The team may have completed the validation of its work as best it can, but its upstream dependencies are unstable, resulting in unstable deliverables to your team.

- The team might be under intense time pressure from customers, partners, or leadership. Perhaps team members are preparing for an important demo or another significant event. The team is rushing its deliverables and lowering its quality to meet the date.

- The team might have lowered its quality standards to meet what team members believe are the norms for the project. They looked at their peer teams and noticed that the overwhelming majority of those teams considers lightly validated code to be good enough to pass along.

Your team may not agree with other teams' practices or definitions, but in the midst of a large project, you're not likely to change how other teams work.

Note Other teams may not like your practice of delivering production-ready scenarios and components. They may want your code earlier, before it's been validated, or in bulk rather than in small batches. They may not appreciate being expected to deliver quality upfront rather than validating work later, during a project-wide stabilization period. You may think other teams are being slow and inefficient (and you're right from a customer-delivery perspective), but given initial low-quality expectations, those same teams may see you as slow and inefficient. These differences can be upsetting to both sides, but remember, you are all in the project together. Collaborating with other teams is a give-and-take.

Even if you can't agree on quality and approach, you can come to a common understanding with your partner teams. Ask each team what you should expect from their deliverables upon handoff. Ask them how they define common terms, like "complete," "done," and "ready." Tell them about what to expect from you and how you define common terms. Post the definitions in an online or physical location where your team members and other teams can see them. Setting clear expectations up front avoids much of the frustration and misunderstandings later in the project.

Tip Describe your definitions of "complete," "done," and "ready" to your partner teams factually, without pride or perceived condescension. It's simply the way you work—not a value judgment. Pride and condescension are often received poorly, whereas a factual description followed by delivery of quality work makes a far better impression. You'll win more fans with modesty and customer value than you will with hubris.

If your upstream dependencies define "complete," "done," and "ready" as code that is implemented but far from production-ready, you'll need to mitigate the problem. Here are a few approaches:

- Treat unstable dependencies as you would late dependencies (described earlier in this section). This includes the options of using a Track column on your signboard, creating fakes or shims, or assisting your upstream partner team with implementation. This approach works best during the early portion of a project, when you've got time to do other work or extra work.

- Implement your work items on top of unstable dependencies, using a combination of fakes and shims to fill in gaps as necessary. You'll need to create a new task for removing the fakes and shims and validate again when your upstream partner teams stabilize the dependencies. This approach is often required late in a project when you can't delay implementation any longer.

- Align your Validate done rule with a lower quality bar. For example, you might replace the rule "The work is deployed to production, tried by a significant subset of real customers, and all issues found are resolved" with "The work is successfully integrated into the main branch, basic test cases function, and all issues found are logged in the bug-tracking system." This passive "When in Rome, do as the Romans do" approach is far from ideal, but in certain situations, it may be the most pragmatic solution.

- Push your upstream partner teams to make their deliverables production-ready. Log bugs for every malfunctioning scenario, feature, story, and component; engage your partner teams on every bug; and drive for resolution on those bugs in time to meet your committed delivery dates. This aggressive approach can be effective, but you'll need executive sponsorship to use it successfully, should your partner teams complain and escalate.

My teams have used all of these approaches at one time or another. My preference is to treat unstable dependencies like late dependencies (the first approach).

Unfortunately, time pressure sometimes forces you to implement on top of unstable dependencies, lower your quality bar, or become a disciplinarian to your upstream partner teams. Those secondary approaches tend to introduce more work and risk to the project. If every team defined "complete" to be production-ready, the same customer value could be delivered without the extra work and risk to your team. However, taking that extra work and risk is worth it to ensure the success of the overall project. Collaborating with other teams on a big project requires flexibility and cooperation.

Inside Xbox

When my teams were responsible for the Microsoft gaming websites, including Xbox.com, we were at the top of the service stack, and thus had many dependencies. The web service teams we depended on used a variety of project-management methods. Sometimes dependencies were delivered to us late or were unreliable.

To account for late or unstable services, we used three approaches:

- Postponed work until our dependencies were functional. In addition to logging the bugs we found against the service teams, we assigned project managers to work closely with service teams, ensuring that they understood our time and quality requirements.

- Created fakes for missing or unstable services. We continued to use these fakes for testing even after the real services came online. Again, we logged bugs and engaged our project managers with the service teams as needed.

- Completed the necessary service work ourselves. We had to do this only in a few cases, when the service teams were lacking resources and our requirements were lower priority than their other work. It was difficult and put stress on the trust between the teams involved. Fortunately, we worked hard to have good relationships with other teams, which served us well.

Toward the end of my time with the gaming websites, we were asked to create online authentication and purchase flows that could be embedded within apps (online webpages hosted within the apps). It was exciting new work and required tight integration with the app teams. Those teams used Scrummerfall and were under an extremely tight schedule. Their definition of complete was that the code worked for basic cases (but was far from production-ready). We worked so closely together that having different definitions of complete wasn't viable. With the tight deadlines, and the app teams driving the schedule, we had to change our Validate done rule to "The basic test cases function, and all issues found are logged in the bug-tracking system." It was uncomfortable, but we shipped on time.

My current teams are near the bottom of the platform and service stacks, so most of our partner teams depend on us. We generally finish our work on time or early, resulting in few problems. In the cases when we do depend on other teams, we treat their late or unstable work as late and track it, or we lean on our strong inter-team relationships and complete the work with them.

Staying productive during stabilization

Toward the end of a large project, there is often a prolonged stabilization period, particularly if many of the teams in the large organization use Scrummerfall or traditional Waterfall. During stabilization, the entire organization focuses exclusively on fixing bugs, doing various forms of system validation, and logging any new or reoccurring bugs that are found. Stabilization for a large project can sometimes take longer than the rest of the project combined, as the result of scenarios and components being finished late with minimal integration testing. Often, entire scenarios, features, and components are removed from the product—which means an enormous amount of effort was wasted, but this step is necessary if the work isn't ready.

On a team using Kanban, you complete features before starting new ones—and the done rules ensure that completed work is always production-ready—even if your peer teams don't. Thus, during a prolonged, organization-wide stabilization period, there are few bugs for your Kanban team to resolve and nothing needs to be cut. However, it's important for your team to stay productive, even when your team has already met the primary objective of stabilization.

Should a bug in your team's area be found during stabilization, it is immediately the top priority. However, during the rest of the time, there are several productive activities for an otherwise idle Kanban team:

- Keep working on new tasks for the current release. This might break project rules, so it may not be an option. You should negotiate with project management and leadership in advance to agree on what work you can continue doing and under what conditions.

- Work on tasks for the next release (or a different project) that are checked in to a different source control branch. This also might break project rules or generate animosity among your peer teams. Often, a few team members can do this without drawing much attention to themselves, while other team members contribute to the current project in other ways.

- Run innovative experiments, create prototypes, and acquire customer feedback. This might generate animosity among your peer teams. Often, a few team members can do this work constructively while they remain sensitive to the hard work others are doing on the current project.

- Improve infrastructure and tooling, and address other technical debt that has been neglected. This kind of work is always welcome and can be easily interrupted should a high-priority bug be found in the current project.

- Train yourself or your team on new techniques and methods. Like improving infrastructure and tooling, self-improvement is an investment that pays dividends.

- Determine the root cause of various issues you've encountered and seek to fix them. This work fits right into stabilization.

- Help other teams stabilize their code, particularly teams you depend on. This option may not be the most alluring, but it's the most helpful and will generate goodwill among your partner teams.

Checklist

Here's a checklist of actions to take when your team uses Kanban within a large organization:

❑ Understand your organization's high-level vision, architecture, and schedule for its upcoming major product release.

❑ Choose how your team will contribute to the high-level vision and fit into the high-level architecture:

- By scenario

- By component

- By component with ownership of small related scenarios (hybrid)

❑ Establish your team's minimum viable product (MVP) within the organization-wide MVP.

❑ Order your team's work in coordination with your peer teams, using automated project-management tools, review meetings relying on work-item system queries, or a socially intensive group meeting.

❑ Fit your ordered deliverables (work items) into the high-level schedule's milestones, using current task estimates (CTE), task add rate (TAR), and task completion rate (TCR).

❑ Determine when and how you will synchronize your Kanban board with your organization's online work-item tracking system.

❑ Select a means to inform the larger organization of when your team completes major deliverables or makes a breaking change to an interface.

❑ Create a Track column under your Implement step for items blocked by late or unstable dependencies.

❑ Add note cards for creating fakes and shims as needed for late or unstable dependencies, and add matching note cards to later remove those fakes and shims.

❑ Meet with your peer teams to discuss how each of your teams define "complete," "done," and "ready," and post those definitions in an online or physical location where your team members and other teams can see them.

❑ Discuss what your team would do if particularly important dependencies are late or unstable.

❑ Plan appropriate and constructive activities for your team during your organization's prolonged stabilization periods.

CHAPTER 8

Sustained engineering

By James Waletzky

Most teams that release a product or service to customers perform software maintenance after release. An effective team minimizes defects during development, but some level of post-ship fixes are inevitable. This situation poses problems even for a mature team in its need to prioritize and schedule unplanned maintenance work in conjunction with developing product road map features (new development). What is an effective model for dealing with this distraction from new feature development, hereafter known as "sustained engineering" (SE)? I'm sure you already guessed— Kanban.

The model I recommend for using Kanban to address post-release defects has several aspects. The teams involved need to define roles and responsibilities (support, product management, and engineering), determine ownership of SE work, and also lay out the support tiers they will use. To address the need for efficient collaboration, teams can use an approach such as triage as well as "quick-solve" meetings to help manage maintenance work that requires escalation. You can put a specific Kanban workflow in place to track escalations and bugs by making use of a signboard and complement this with other appropriate tracking tools, both physical and software. I'll explore each aspect of this model throughout this chapter.

The topics covered are:

Define terms, goals, and roles
Determine SE ownership
Lay out support tiers
Collaborate for efficiency
Implement Kanban SE workflow
Kanban tools
Troubleshooting
Checklist

Define terms, goals, and roles

Before I address how Kanban helps with sustained engineering, in this section I provide some context about several topics that teams need to consider. First, I list several terms that need a common understanding in SE to help ensure that they are used consistently across support, development, and SE teams. Next, I list some of the challenges and goals that organizations face when doing SE so that you can see how Kanban helps. Finally, I describe the roles and responsibilities that need to be clarified so that different teams have a shared view of who is involved.

Consistent vocabulary

The following terms and definitions provide a common vocabulary to use across teams:

Term	Definition
Bug/defect	A deviation from expected product behavior. Bugs may be fixed by the core engineering team and the fixes deployed to users.
Core engineering team	A cross-functional team consisting of business analysts/program managers, software developers, QA engineers, user experience engineers, and anyone else who contributes to shipping a product or service.
Escalation	An incident that is not easily solved by a customer-support person and requires assistance from the core engineering team.
Hotfix	A bug fix that is typically deployed to a small number of customers shortly after it is discovered.
Incident	A customer-reported issue with the software. The customer-support team owns incidents and manages their outcomes.
Service pack, update	A set of bug fixes and hotfixes that are deployed as one unit. Service packs are used less frequently by teams that release regularly.
Support tiers	Customer-support organizations are typically segmented by tiers. Tier 1 handles the first contact with customers and the overall tracking of incidents. Tier 2 may own longer-running investigations, and tier 3 represents a technical team that does lower-level detailed investigation.

Challenges and goals

Engineering teams typically have the following challenges when dealing with post-ship bugs:

- Customer issues take too long to resolve because of many competing (and sometimes changing) priorities.

- Work is difficult to prioritize. How does a team choose between working on customer issues and moving the product road map forward?

- Unplanned maintenance work is challenging to predict and schedule. If release-date predictability is a goal of your organization, it is important to predict how much time the team will spend on fixing bugs versus adding new functionality.

- The customer-support team lacks visibility into the work of the core engineering team. After an issue moves to the core engineering team, the customer-support team wants to be kept informed of the state of the issue.

- Engineering teams work in a silo. Collaboration with companion teams (such as customer support) doesn't happen on a regular basis.

- The core engineering team is not motivated to fix bugs. Developers are typically attracted to creating new functionality and solving new problems. Bug fixes are not viewed as a "fun" task.

By putting Kanban in place, you can address challenges such as those I outline. The goals for the SE practice, and how Kanban helps in each case, include the following:

- **Minimize team distractions**   By having the sustained-engineering role clarified, with the right responsibilities in place, the team efficiently deals with escalations and minimizes distractions.

- **Make quick decisions**   As you have seen in previous chapters, Kanban does not include a planning meeting. Escalations are placed in an ordered list as they come in, so customer-support personnel, and potentially users, can see how their issues are prioritized.

- **Fix the right issues the right way**   A forced stack-ranked board of work items ensures that the team is always working on what is most important. The done rules inherent to the Kanban workflow influence quality.

- **Visualize work in progress**   Anyone with access to the signboard can quickly see which issues are at the top of the priority list, in progress, or done.

- **Minimize work in progress**   As described earlier, the work-in-progress (WIP) limits Kanban imposes ensure that the core engineering team is working on a focused set of issues instead of continually working on issues randomly and never finishing.

- **Deliver frequently**   Customer issues require quick turnaround. Within a software as a service (SaaS) model, fixes can be deployed rapidly, solving issues for multiple customers at a time. The overall flow of a Kanban system facilitates frequent releases.

- **Measure sustained-engineering effectiveness**   Kanban surfaces a set of metrics that you can use to measure how well your team is doing in dealing with escalations. These metrics are visible to all stakeholders.

- **Improve collaboration with customer support**   Through a process that sits alongside the Kanban workflow, the core engineering team works more directly with support, accounting for user issues and collaboratively prioritizing work.

- **Improve team motivation**   Because the overall process is visible and outputs are measured, the motivation to drive issues to completion as efficiently as possible increases.

How are these goals met? It starts with having the right team and the right people in the right place.

Define roles and responsibilities

Here are the key stakeholders and their responsibilities in the sustained-engineering process:

- **Customer support**   This team has a direct interface with customers and is ultimately responsible for any issues that are reported. The support team works with a representative from the core engineering team on any escalations that need to be addressed.

- **Product management**   The product management (PM) team owns the product road map and the prioritization of any incoming requests to the engineering team. The person who filters requests to the engineering team may be a member of the team itself (such as a business analyst or program manager).

- **Core engineering team**   The cross-functional team consisting of business analysts/program managers, software developers, QA engineers, user experience engineers, and anyone else who contributes to shipping the product or service. The core engineering team is responsible for detailed analysis of issues.

Determine SE ownership

The first area to consider is whether to have a dedicated SE team in place, appoint a dedicated SE person on the core engineering team, or leave the responsibility for SE with the core engineering team. Each decision has advantages and disadvantages.

- **Dedicated SE team**   Having a team of people whose sole responsibility is to deal with support escalations and post-ship issues allows the core engineering team to focus exclusively on marching forward. In this model, the core engineering team's Kanban board contains minimal distractions. However, being a full-time member of an SE team might be viewed as less glorious than being a member of the core engineering team, and SE team members may have lower motivation to succeed. As a result, the right personal and systemic incentives must be in place and the team must be an important part of an organization's culture. Helpful staffing strategies include initiating new hires through their inclusion on the SE team for a set number of weeks or months, rotating members of the core engineering team to the SE team, or hiring full-time members.

> **Tip** I recommend starting new hires on the SE team to familiarize them with the product and having an intermediate to senior member of the core engineering team rotate through as the technical leader of the SE team to provide mentoring and coaching. Some engineers find that they love the challenge of continuous problem solving and want to remain on the SE team.

- **Dedicated SE person**   This person is part of the core engineering team but has the sole responsibility of handling escalations and does not work on product enhancements. An advantage of this model is that the same team works on cleaning up post-ship issues that they likely created. Additionally, the dedicated SE person is ingrained in the team and can quickly get help. However, this role may not be coveted. A rotation program with incentives can help.

- **Core engineering team ownership**   In this model, incoming escalations are ranked on the signboard along with the team's other tasks. One advantage of this model is that issues are addressed by the most knowledgeable people. Also, the team feels the pain of post-ship issues and is motivated to prevent them. A disadvantage is that the team can be frequently distracted by escalations, preventing it from making forward progress on the feature road map.

I've used two models depending on the circumstances:

- With a core engineering team that is just getting started with Kanban and is maintaining a large load of technical debt (including bugs and refactoring tasks), start with a dedicated SE team until quality is under control. This model allows the core engineering team to reduce the debt while the team improves its development practices to minimize future issues. It also ingrains good habits into engineers who later move to the core engineering team. Meanwhile, the rest of the engineering staff can continue to deliver new value for customers.

- For a team that has manageable technical debt, I prefer the model in which the core engineering team retains ownership. This model encourages personal accountability for quality along with broad improvements instead of spot fixes.

Now that the right team structure and roles are in place, how does Kanban work for sustained engineering? Let's look at how all the moving parts work together.

Lay out support tiers

Medium-to-large organizations typically have up to three levels of support to provide the best customer experience and minimize distractions to the core engineering team. Figure 8-1 shows this model and a typical workflow. I'll focus on the operations that occur in tier 3, when incidents are escalated to the core engineering team.

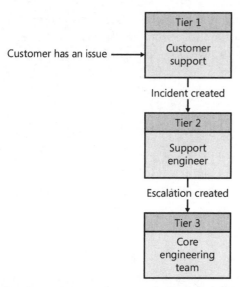

FIGURE 8-1 A model of a three-tier customer-support operation.

Tier 1

A customer calls, emails, or chats with a customer-support representative and reports an issue with the product. A support incident is created. If the incident is addressed in real time, the incident is closed and does not move on to the next tiers.

Tier 2

Incidents that require follow-up after the initial request are handled with a longer-term engagement, perhaps by a support engineer, with the history of the request reflected in the incident. This engagement might include follow-up phone calls or emails, analysis of log files, and the retrieval of other troubleshooting data. If more in-depth technical investigation is required, the incident is escalated to tier 3, which typically involves the core engineering team.

Tier 3

If an incident finds its way to the core engineering team through an escalation, it is time to track the work in the engineering work-tracking system. For a Kanban team using a paper-based signboard, the incident makes its way onto the physical signboard. For a Kanban team using a project tracking tool, a new work item is created and tied back to the incident in the customer-support system. At this point, however, the new work is not yet ranked (see the next section, "Collaborate for efficiency," for details).

> **Note** Smaller organizations might have only two tiers of support—an external-facing support tier that works directly with customers, and the core engineering team for help with more technical issues. As the business grows and the core engineering team has to handle a higher volume of support requests, a third tier may be created between the first two. Before taking this step, however, it is important to look at the reasons why the core engineering team is so distracted. For example, is there a general quality issue that could be addressed to help minimize support requests?

Collaborate for efficiency

SE requires collaboration across roles for maximum efficiency. Two structured techniques that help facilitate collaboration include triage meetings and quick-solve meetings.

Triage

The term *triage* comes from the medical industry. It refers to the steps that personnel in an emergency room take to assess the criticality of patient injuries to determine which patients take precedence for treatment. The triage of incoming incidents is a best practice for software teams to determine which issues require the core engineering team's attention and in what priority.

I recommend that a triage team review all escalations before the core engineering team begins work on any of those issues to ensure that the most important issues receive attention first.

> **Note** Triage is derived from the French *trier*, which means "to sort." The term can be traced back to the late 1700s, when a French military surgeon, Baron Dominique-Jean Larrey, developed a system for prioritizing casualties on the battlefield during the Crimean War. (See *https://en.wikipedia.org/wiki/Dominique_Jean_Larrey*.) The concept involved treating the most urgent cases first, where survival was feasible, regardless of whether the wounded were still on the battlefield. As the concept evolved, cases were pushed through a work-flow in which doctors more equipped to handle the care took over. With software, the analogy fits well. An individual or team is initially in charge of prioritizing cases, and then other teams, such as the development team, take over in applicable cases and resolve the issues.

The triage team typically consists of a representative of the customer-support team, a product manager (or business analyst or program manager), a development leader, and a QA leader. The primary goal of the triage team is to prevent distractions for the core engineering team. Specifically, the triage team does the following:

- Answers workaround and resolution feasibility questions without involving the rest of the core engineering team.

- Removes any duplicate escalations.

- Validates that enough data is supplied with the escalation.

- Stack-ranks any incoming escalations on the Kanban board.

- Recommends the release vehicle for any escalations that are immediately deemed bugs, such as a customer hotfix or general service pack.

- Ensures cross-team synchronization on new escalations as well as any escalations currently in progress.

Triage meetings typically take place twice per week, but they may be held more or less frequently depending on the number or severity of incoming escalations. Immediately after a product is shipped, the number of escalations may be larger as the support team learns the details of the product or quality issues are discovered.

Following the triage meeting, the new work item is stack ranked in the appropriate position on the signboard.

In the same way that your team might have a "requirement" or "user story" work-item type on either its physical signboard or in the project-management software you use, I recommend that you also have an "escalation" work-item type. This practice allows for tracking metrics related to product confusion versus actual quality issues.

Note At Microsoft, triage is engrained into the culture. Every team I worked on did triage at varying frequencies, with as many as two triage meetings per day for internally discovered issues as the release date approached. The odds are that you won't find a single person on a Microsoft engineering team who does not have a clear definition of what triage means. I recommend that you build the practice into your culture.

Quick-solve meeting

The goal of a quick-solve meeting is to augment triage by rapidly reducing the queue of escalations before the core engineering team starts to work on them. You can think of this meeting as a kind of "tier 2.5" level of support. Whereas the goal of the triage meeting is to ensure that sufficient information is available for ranking and addressing an escalation, the goal of the quick-solve meeting is to *quickly resolve* any escalations that do not require code changes.

Quick-solve discussions should not last longer than five minutes per item. This meeting's participants are similar to those who attend the triage meeting, although it is recommended that an additional subject matter expert (a developer or QA engineer who is very familiar with the technical and functional aspects of the product) be included. A cadence of one quick-solve meeting per week is reasonable to help prevent distractions later in the workflow.

Implement Kanban SE workflow

A core engineering team might choose to track escalations and bugs on its overall Kanban board. However, a Kanban board used to track a dedicated sustained-engineering team looks a little different. The focus of the signboard is on escalations and bugs instead of on specifying new product behavior. In the high-level view of the signboard shown in the following illustration, escalations are separated from bugs (by using a second row) to reflect that they are different work-item types with a slightly different workflow. An escalation might not become a bug, and a bug does not necessarily have an escalation.

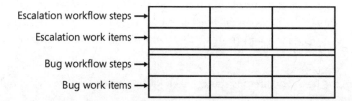

Work usually starts as an escalation and runs through the pull system until the issue is determined to be a product bug or has been answered appropriately and closed. A product bug is created if necessary, in which case the item starts over in the bugs row.

The workflow described in the following sections is based on having a dedicated sustained-engineering team in place, but the concepts apply regardless of which model of ownership you use.

Escalations

A typical signboard for SE escalations looks something like this:

Escalations		Investigate (4)	Done
☐	☐	☐	☐
☐	☐		☐
☐	☐		☐
☐	☐		

This signboard also looks a little different from those shown in previous chapters—with new names and only one step—but it acts just the same. As noted in previous chapters, it is extremely important to define when an item is ready to be moved from one column to another (the done rule).

The Escalations backlog is the stack-ranked list of escalations that have been triaged, which is a prerequisite for inserting an item in this list. The team pulls items off this list as team members are ready to begin investigating the next item (assuming that the WIP limit allows for additional work).

The Investigate column tracks which issues are actively being investigated. Typical activities include clarifying the escalation, attempting to reproduce a problem, and identifying a suitable workaround. The Investigate done rule, which completes an escalation, is "Incident-tracking system updated with investigation results; customer notified; tasks to avoid future incidents created (such as writing a knowledge base article); and any resulting product bugs added to the second row of the signboard." Modify your own done rule as you need to.

Bugs/Other Work

A typical signboard for SE bugs looks something like this:

Bugs/Other		Develop (3)	Validate (3)	Root-cause analysis (3)	Waiting	Deployed
☐	☐	☐☐	☐	☐	☐	☐
☐			☐	☐		☐
☐			☐			☐

The Bugs/Other backlog is the stack-ranked list of bugs to address. The source of a bug is a previous escalation or a bug that was added directly to this backlog after triage. Note the "Other" classification. An example of a work item in the Other category is a small product improvement (such as improved logging in the software) that would make sustained engineering more effective. A second example is an operational improvement, such as a diagnostics tool, that makes the team more efficient.

The Develop column reflects the work a developer or QA engineer needs to do to address the issue. For post-ship bugs, it is strongly recommended that an automated test be in place that validates the fix before work is pulled into the Validate column. It is probable that a test for the issue did not exist before, and increasing test coverage over time is a best practice.

I recommend using a test-driven development approach to address bugs. First, write a unit test (or an integration test) that exercises intended behavior. This test should fail because of the presence of the bug. Next, fix the bug, and then run the test again. It should pass this time. Finally, refactor as necessary to clean up the code around the fix. This approach is not always feasible with legacy code that is not designed to be easily tested, but you should make a low-risk best effort. The Develop done rule is, "All relevant unit tests pass, including new unit test(s) that validate the fix; fixes are 'buddy tested' on a separate machine (typically by QA); and integration tests are enhanced as appropriate to exercise the exposed area."

The Validate column indicates that a member of the team—likely a QA engineer—needs to validate the acceptance criteria for the bug by running a set of acceptance tests on an automated build. (You do have an automated build, right?) The Validate done rule is, "All acceptance criteria met and any issues found are resolved."

A root-cause analysis exercise is undertaken to determine why a bug escaped the defenses of the core engineering team. This exercise identifies operational improvements that could prevent similar bugs from being released to customers in the future. This exercise could be part of your Develop or Validate done rule, but I prefer to have a specific step in the workflow to make the practice explicit. Examples of improvements include a more rigorous acceptance criteria definition, modification of development practices such as code review or unit testing procedures, testing in a staging area that mirrors production, or including a user acceptance test stage before releasing to a wider audience. The act of practicing continuous improvement is often called *kaizen* in Lean and Agile development circles.

> **Note** *Kaizen* is a Japanese term meaning "good change," but it is often translated as "continuous improvement," particularly in the business world. Kaizen involves observing a problem, ideally with metrics such as cycle time, determining the root cause of the problem, making a change to address it, monitoring and measuring the results, and infinitely repeating. Building a kaizen mentality into your team culture is recommended and is often done with small changes on a daily basis at both a personal and team level.

Improvements might be identified with a simple root-cause analysis process such as the "5 Whys" (*http://en.wikipedia.org/wiki/5_Whys*) or, my personal favorite, the Six Boxes (*http://www.sixboxes .com*). The Six Boxes provide a root-cause analysis and solution framework that helps you look above and beyond the obvious symptoms by focusing on expectations and feedback, tools and processes, incentives, motivation, selection and assignment (or capacity), and skills and knowledge. The root-cause analysis done rule is, "Analysis complete and recommended actions are inserted back into the SE team's backlog or fed back to the core engineering team for inclusion in their backlog."

The Waiting section indicates that completed bugs and other code-based work items are done and part of an official build but are waiting for a release vehicle. A bug may be released on its own or may be deployed with a combination of other work. When work items are live, they are moved to the Deployed section. You might consider triggering a release based on the number of items in the Waiting section.

As with any Kanban implementation, there is no one right way to define the workflow. The one presented in this section is a recommended starting point, but feel free to customize it to meet your process. The signboard might be set up differently, for example, depending on your SE ownership model. With ownership in the core engineering team, you might want to track all of the team's work in one place. Additionally, a separate signboard might be too much overhead and you might choose to have escalations and work items distinguished by the color of your note cards or a symbol on the cards.

Kanban tools

As described in Chapter 2, "Kanban quick-start guide," a physical signboard is the best tool for visualizing workflow. However, a software tool can complement the physical signboard in certain circumstances—for example, when a team has a desire to use a bug-tracking system, to facilitate communication across teams, to meet a company-wide mandate, or when a distributed team does not interact in person every day.

An example of a tool you can use for these purposes is Microsoft Team Foundation Server (TFS). TFS provides a reasonable method of visualizing a signboard, but you may be restricted in producing an exact representation of your physical signboard. Some customizations are possible, such as the creation of an Escalation work item. Tools such as JIRA provide similar capabilities.

Any tool must make your life easier and more efficient, or why bother using it. I recommend that you implement Kanban in the same work-item tracking system as you use for other development work. For example, recording bugs in a defect-tracking system that's separate from your other work would create inefficiencies and duplication. Most redundancy is evil per the DRY principle—"Don't Repeat Yourself."

Ideally, the customer-support system and engineering work-item tracking system are integrated such that the original incident and the escalated work item can be tied together. This lets customer support see the state of the work item as the core engineering team works on it, and the core engineering team can see updates made by the support team. Why not use the same system for both customer support and development? The needs of the two teams are different.

The customer-support system is more external facing and tracks a different data set than the internal system. For example, an external system notes customer contact information, whereas an internal system focuses on when the fix is deployed and how it is tested. Depending on your various systems, an integrator/plug-in may be available to integrate the two. In the worst case, most of these types of systems have a documented API, and the SE team could develop a bridge to tie them together. This integration could be a fun project for the SE team to take on.

If your team wants to use a physical signboard (recommended), but the organization mandates tracking work items in a software tool, try to prevent redundancy:

1. Print the contents of your software-tracked work items onto physical cards and attach those to your wall, window, or whiteboard for tracking.

2. Appoint one person to ensure that the work items in the software system are updated after the team does its daily standup.

Troubleshooting

This section covers some common issues that can cause trouble using Kanban for sustained engineering.

Problem: The core engineering team is inundated with escalations from customer support, creating an unsustainable backlog

Kanban provides an easy visualization of the number of escalations and bugs that a team must deal with. An excessive number of escalations may indicate one or more problems:

- The support team relies too much on the core engineering team. Use the triage team to help shield the core engineering team from distractions and to ensure that only the appropriate escalations get through.

- Difficult escalations result in long lead times. Aim to improve diagnostic tools (such as tracing and logging) to help resolve more technical problems.

- Insufficient help or documentation for customers and the support organization. The core engineering team should spend a reasonable amount of time prior to release educating stakeholders on new functionality.

- Post-ship product-quality issues. In the spirit of continuous improvement, work with the core engineering team to refine their processes and improve early cycle quality.

Problem: We are a new SE team and have no idea what to set the WIP limits to

Just start with *something*. Discuss as a team and agree on the first cut at WIP limits. Over time, adjust the WIP limits on the basis of your experience until team members agree that they have found reasonable values. Consider holding periodic retrospectives to continuously improve your team's practices, and refine the WIP limits as part of those retrospectives. (You can find more information about troubleshooting WIP limits in the "Troubleshooting" section in Chapter 2.)

Problem: The Waiting section on the signboard has a large number of items

Fortunately, you are using Kanban, so unreleased fixes become visible quickly. Perhaps the team needs to consider more frequent releases in the form of higher cadence deployments or additional downloadable updates. If more frequent releases involve issues such as the absence of automated deployment steps, prioritize operational improvements to remove those bottlenecks. If the SE team's finished work items are not getting to customers quickly, the great work that the SE team is doing to keep customers happy is not fully realized.

Problem: The customer-support team is continuously querying the core engineering team for predicted completion dates for open issues

The engineering team should be as transparent as possible with its progress on open escalations. The team's work is visualized through the signboard, and all stakeholders are encouraged to provide input about the ranking of work items. The customer-support team can pull updates from the SE team whenever they like. Also, by having a customer-support representative on the triage team, collaboration between support and development is frequent and more effective, giving support input into the stack ranking. Knowing that the SE team is using Kanban, the support team is confident that issues will be addressed as quickly as possible.

To further improve the predictability of escalation completion dates, simply measure the average lead time of the work items. Lead time can be measured in various ways, such as the duration between the opening and closing of customer support tickets, or the duration between the addition of the escalation to the core engineering team's backlog and the deployment of the fix. To keep things simple, take a sample of work items from the past few weeks, compute the average lead time, and use that number as the basis for predicting completion dates. You can use more advanced statistical methods by plotting a histogram of lead-time ranges that account for different types of work items and then analyzing the distribution of those lead times to determine more accurate delivery rates. This type of analysis is good input for a service level agreement (SLA) to create a high-confidence contract for expected escalation and issue-resolution times.

Problem: The team is having problems planning for maintenance because it doesn't know how many escalations will come its way

Many teams struggle with unplanned work. This is the primary reason why Kanban is such a great model—there is less need to plan for an iteration; instead, accept unpredictability and stack-rank accordingly. Large backlogs of items might require you and others to set expectations, but a transparent backlog and signboard help shed light on the capacity and throughput of the core engineering team.

Problem: A dedicated SE team is fixing issues but creating more bugs with every fix

Legacy code can be brittle and lack automated regression tests. When one item is fixed, the risk of breaking other pieces of code is high. To mitigate this risk, do the following:

- Rotate a developer from the core engineering team to the SE team to help transfer technical knowledge to other team members.

- Ask the core engineering team to hold brown-bag learning sessions to help transfer knowledge.

- Practice the test-driven development style for fixing bugs (described earlier), building up unit tests over time, which helps minimize the risk as more tests are added.

- Allocate the time of a more senior member of the core engineering team to participate in code reviews for the more risky fixes done by the SE team.

Problem: Developers are not motivated to fix bugs in an SE role and morale on the team is low

Working in a sustained-engineering role might not be viewed as glamorous work, even though the role is extremely important to the customer satisfaction for any organization. Some ways to help include the following:

- Communicate the importance of the SE team from the highest levels of leadership, along with the benefits of having the greatest impact on customer satisfaction and customer retention.

- Start new hires on the SE team, which helps keep motivation and morale high.

- Document the overall contribution of the team to the business. The Kanban board makes visibility easier. The SE team gets to know customers better than the core engineering team because of its relationship with customer support.

- Market the team as a fantastic way to get to know both the product and the customers. Learning the breadth of a product or product portfolio is very beneficial (and challenging) for any developer.

- Give the team a fun name and pose challenges to decrease lead time and cycle time for SE issues. For example, a team I worked with named itself after noble gases (Argon, for example) because of the team's ability to keep calm under pressure from customers.

- Create a vision and mission that the team can rally behind.

- Include fun projects on the backlog, particularly when the volume of escalations and bugs is low. This allows for operational improvements that do not affect just the SE team's work but also help improve the core engineering team. The core engineering team will love the SE team for this work, and the relationship will flourish.

- Add small feature requests to the SE backlog if they add functionality to the product in a somewhat isolated way, such as through a plug-in model.

> **Note** At Microsoft, the Windows customer experience team (also known as "Windows sustained engineering") has started to task developers not only with fixing critical issues, but with adding small features that, in particular, enhance the usability of the operating system—for example, making it easier to turn on and off specific functionality that was otherwise very difficult to find buried in the system settings.

Problem: Some of the team members tune out in the daily standup because they are not all working on the same product

An organization with a portfolio of products has to support them all. It may be less effective to have an SE team consisting of developers working on different products, unless each developer works on them all. Instead, consider segmenting the larger SE team into smaller ones, each with its own Kanban board.

Checklist

Here's a checklist of actions to take when your team uses Kanban for sustained engineering (SE):

- ❏ Establish a common vocabulary so that terms such as "escalation" and "incident" are used consistently.

- ❏ Define and document the roles and responsibilities of customer support, product management, and the core engineering team for effective collaboration.

- ❏ Determine SE ownership, using either a dedicated SE team, a dedicated SE person on the core engineering team, or by having the core engineering team stack-rank escalations with its other work (work unrelated to sustained engineering).

- ❏ Define support tiers to clarify the escalation workflow and collaboration between the support team, the SE team, and the core engineering team.

- ❏ Triage incoming escalations to minimize distractions for the SE engineers so that they work on only the issues that matter.

- ❏ Use quick-solve meetings to rapidly reduce the queue of escalations that do not require code changes.

- ❏ Implement a SE workflow using Kanban. Track escalations in the top half of the signboard and bugs and other code work in the lower half of the signboard.

- ❏ Clearly define your done rules for the Kanban workflow.

❏ Practice kaizen (continuous improvement) by doing root-cause analysis when bugs are fixed to prevent similar errors in the future.

❏ Use work-item management tools where necessary, but give preference to a physical signboard. Tools that integrate the customer-support system and engineering work-item tracking systems can help.

CHAPTER 9

Further resources and beyond

Previous chapters have introduced you to Kanban. You can plan and hit deadlines with Kanban. You can use Kanban to adapt from traditional Waterfall or evolve from Scrum. You can continuously integrate and push components, continuously publish apps and content, and continuously deploy services. You can even use Kanban within large projects and organizations and for sustained engineering.

Once you've gotten a real sense of Kanban, a few questions may occur to you:

- Can I use Kanban for everything I do?

- What practices are and aren't compatible with Kanban?

- Why does Kanban work so well?

- How can I improve beyond Kanban?

This chapter provides an overview of further resources to expand your use and understanding of Kanban and to help you go beyond Kanban to improve your business and life.

The topics covered are:

Expanding Kanban to new areas of business and life
Mixing Agile and Lean with Kanban
Why Kanban works
Improving beyond Kanban
Checklist

Expanding Kanban to new areas of business and life

Can you use Kanban for everything you do? Kanban can be useful for a broad range of activities in your business and personal life. The primary requirement is that the work have a start and an end. You can use Kanban for teams as large as the room having your signboard will hold or just by yourself.

I'll start with business applications and end with personal Kanban.

Scaling Kanban up, down, and out

You can scale Kanban up to work with as many people as can fit in a room to view the signboard during daily standup. At a practical level, that's less than 100 people. Kanban scales up well because individuals can move their own cards at any time, not everyone needs to speak at the daily standup meetings (only those with blocking issues), and Kanban's flow fits nicely with today's service-oriented architectures. If you use a virtual signboard online, you can include even more people in the daily standup, but the number and variety of note cards on the signboard will eventually become unmanageable. When your signboard becomes unwieldy, or your architecture dictates a significant refactoring, it's time to split up the team.

See also *Anderson, David J.* Kanban. *Sequim, WA: Blue Hole Press, 2010.*

As you apply Kanban to manage larger teams, you'll likely encounter a wider variety of work and types of work items. Each type of work item might have a different set of steps to complete it. You can see a small example of this in Chapter 8, "Sustained engineering," where the signboard has two swim lanes (also sometimes called "pipelines"): one for escalations and one for bugs. Each swim lane has its own steps with their own WIP limits and done rules. The swim lanes appear on the same board, stacked on top of each other, as shown in Chapter 8. Some boards might display five or six different swim lanes. In the Kanban quick-start guide (Chapter 2), I keep things simple by having different work-item types share the same steps within a single swim lane. However, with larger teams and a wide variety of work, separate swim lanes may be necessary to properly track work variation.

See also *Ladas, Corey.* Scrumban: Essays on Kanban Systems for Lean Software Development. *Modus Cooperandi, 2009.*

Adding swim lanes to your signboard expands it down, but you can also expand Kanban out—upstream and downstream in your workflow. Most of the signboard examples shown in this book have three steps: Specify, Implement, and Validate. However, your signboard can reflect the unique steps in your product development, including the steps prior to specification and the steps following validation. In other words, you can have a single Kanban board for your product from end to end.

I cover many of the steps following validation in Chapter 6, "Deploying components, apps, and services," but I assume that those steps are happening outside your small team, so your signboard only needs to track them. If your team is responsible for its own deployments, you can add the deployment steps to your signboard with appropriate WIP limits and done rules.

My favorite steps that start prior to specification are from Scenario-Focused Engineering (SFE). Here's what an SFE signboard might look like:

- The Backlog column contains high-level initiatives, each of which is a desired outcome for a target customer segment, such as "Immersive holographic environment for gamers" (a fictitious example).

- The Observe step takes a high-level initiative and observes the target customers, capturing everything about who they are, what they do, how they act, and why they care. The Observe done rule might be, "Captured mix of quantitative, qualitative, seeing, and doing customer data, and documented insights from that data."

- The Frame step takes customer data and insights and uses them to frame a series of success metrics and SPICIER scenarios. (SPICIER stands for "tells a customer **S**tory," "includes **P**ersonal details," "is **I**mplementation-free," "told in the **C**ustomer's voice," "reveals deep **I**nsight about customer needs," "includes **E**motion and **E**nvironment," and "is based on **R**esearch.") The Frame done rule might be, "Produced a prioritized collection of SPICIER scenarios with associated success metrics."

- The Brainstorm step takes a scenario and brainstorms all the different ways it could be brought to life. The choices that best fulfill the scenario and meet the requirements are considered for prototyping. The Brainstorm done rule might be, "Generated a dozen or more alternatives, and settled on three to five promising designs."

- The Prototype step takes a design and rapidly conjures a prototype sufficient for customer feedback. That prototype could be a paper model, a PowerPoint animation, or a simple code change that can be the subject of A/B testing. The expectation is that your first guess won't be quite right, so you want to spend just a few days on two or three variations and then get customer feedback. The Prototype done rule might be, "Captured customer feedback on one or more related prototypes." Conceptually, note cards from prototyping might move back to the Brainstorm column or earlier if customer feedback indicates that more design work is needed. (In practice, you typically create new cards with a slightly different focus.)

- The Breakdown step is basically the Specify step from the Kanban quick-start guide (Chapter 2), but here much of the specification is already provided by the previously created scenarios, designs, prototypes, and customer feedback. The Breakdown done rule might be, "All items broken down to less than a week of work each, with specification materials available."

- The remaining Implement and Validate steps are as described in the Kanban quick-start guide. You could also add on sections at the end to track deployments as described in Chapter 6. Once your product or service is deployed, you can get more customer feedback on working code, which is then fed back in for observation, framing, and brainstorming new ideas.

Scenario-Focused Engineering relies heavily on iteration and customer feedback to adjust designs, prototype new ideas, and hone in on the optimal design. Kanban's continuous delivery and continuous customer feedback is ideally suited for SFE.

See also *De Bonte, Austina, and Drew Fletcher.* Scenario-Focused Engineering: A Toolbox for Innovation and Customer-Centricity. *Redmond, WA: Microsoft Press, 2014.*

Personal Kanban

Many personal projects have a start and an end, including home maintenance, school assignments, and blog entries. If you find yourself needing a little more structure to stay focused and complete these personal tasks, consider Personal Kanban.

In its simplest form, Personal Kanban consists of a small corkboard or whiteboard at home, placed where you'll see it (like in your kitchen). The signboard lists your backlog and has a single step called "Doing," as shown here:

You write items you need to do on sticky notes or note cards and place them in your backlog. You set a limit for how many items should be in progress at once, which becomes your WIP limit for the Doing step. In the example, I set the limit to three, which is enough to keep me busy, but not so many that I lose focus. When you finish an item, you move it from the left column of Doing to the right column, Done. This frees up a spot under Doing, as shown in the example. You can then pull the next item from your backlog and begin doing it.

With Personal Kanban, your daily standup meeting is just you—there's no project manager or analyst to help you order your backlog or manage your workflow. Large backlogs of items can seem overwhelming and unwieldy. To reduce the "existential overhead," it's helpful to add a Next column to your backlog. That way, you always know what's next and can replenish the Next column from the backlog as needed.

Personal Kanban keeps your to-do list organized and tracked in a simple way. It limits how much you're doing at once, which keeps you focused. It also makes your work clearly visible to others and offers that satisfying feeling of moving items to the Done column. There are even Personal Kanban apps for many devices.

If you want to be more sophisticated, you can introduce more steps, separate swim lanes and steps for different types of tasks, and done rules for steps. You can also keep it simple with just the Doing step. It's your personal signboard to help you remain efficient and productive.

See also Benson, Jim, and Tonianne DeMaria Barry. Personal Kanban: Mapping Work | Navigating Life. Seattle: CreateSpace Independent Publishing Platform, 2011.

Mixing Agile and Lean with Kanban

What practices are and aren't compatible with Kanban? Since Kanban is a method to manage workflow, any of the practices that can be thought of as steps in your workflow or as conditions of completing steps in your workflow fit nicely with Kanban. Practices that exist outside a workflow, such as the ad hoc answering of email or freeform meetings, can be adapted to Kanban by creating an email or meeting workflow, but it's excessive to force workflows on everything.

Kanban is one of a collection of Agile and Lean practices. Many of these practices can be used in combination with one another and with Kanban. I've mentioned a few already, like cross-functional teams, continuous integration, iterative development, backlogs, and planning poker.

Here are several other well-known practices, with a brief discussion of how your team can incorporate them into Kanban:

- **Test-driven development (TDD)**   TDD is the practice of writing unit tests for code changes before changing the actual code (as mentioned in Chapter 8). The tests fail initially until the code is written to make them pass. Making tests pass provides positive reinforcement for unit testing. (In contrast, writing code and then writing unit tests that fail negatively reinforces unit testing.) In addition, code written using TDD is testable by design and implements only what's tested, so it tends to have high coherence and loose coupling and does the minimum necessary to meet requirements—all attributes of well-designed code.

  You can leave the use of TDD up to team members if you want to (relying on healthy peer pressure). If you prefer to ingrain TDD into your Kanban workflow, you could call the Implement step "TDD" or make the Implement done rule something like, "Code is developed using TDD and reviewed, the static analysis is clean, the code is checked in, and the customer-facing documentation is complete." (You could also have steps named "Write a unit test" and "Make it pass" on your Kanban board, but that's probably too fine grained because each note card would be a single unit test or small set of tests.)

  See also Beck, Kent. Test-Driven Development by Example. *Boston: Addison-Wesley, 2003.*

- **Refactoring**   Refactoring is the practice of restructuring code without changing its external behavior (unit tests still pass). When a function or class needs to enhance or alter its responsibilities, you can make the class or function bigger and more complex, or you can refactor it (break it up in one of a variety of ways) and then add the new responsibilities while maintaining the coherence of each piece. Refactoring leaves code easier to test, enhance, and maintain. It does require excellent unit testing in advance to ensure that the external behavior after the refactoring is unchanged (no bugs were introduced). Refactoring is an intrinsic part of TDD because you often need to refactor the code after writing a new test.

  You could add a Refactor step prior to Implement, but since refactoring often happens multiple times during implementation, a better choice might be to alter the Implement done rule to be, "Code is written [using TDD], unit tested, refactored as needed, and reviewed; the static analysis is clean; the code is checked in; and the customer-facing documentation is complete."

  See also Fowler, Martin, et al. Refactoring: Improving the Design of Existing Code. *Reading, MA: Addison-Wesley, 1999.*

- **Acceptance test-driven development (ATDD)**   ATDD is the practice of writing acceptance tests for new functionality before writing the actual functionality. It's similar to TDD, except it's done at a higher abstraction level. In addition to ensuring that you have a broad set of acceptance tests, ATDD drives clarity in your scenario, story, and feature specifications. After all, it's hard to write acceptance tests without clear acceptance criteria.

ATDD fits well as an additional step on your Kanban board. You might name the steps after Backlog as "Write Acceptance Test," "Breakdown," "Implement," and "Validate." The "Write Acceptance Test" done rule might be, "Acceptance test(s) written, with all success criteria clearly specified." The Breakdown step is basically the Specify step from the Kanban quick-start guide (Chapter 2), but with much of the specification already provided by the acceptance test or tests. The Breakdown done rule might be, "All items broken down to less than a week of work each."

See also *Pugh, Ken.* Lean-Agile Acceptance Test-Driven Development: Better Software Through Collaboration. *Upper Saddle River, NJ: Addison-Wesley, 2011.*

- **Behavior-driven development (BDD)**   BDD is an approach to TDD and ATDD that focuses the tests you write on expected behavior of the unit and system. BDD specifies product behavior in a way that can be easily and clearly verified, often employing specific language to describe tests and the validation of those tests.

  BDD would alter the Kanban done rules you use. If you use ATDD, the "Write Acceptance Test" done rule might be, "Acceptance test(s) written using BDD and obeying BDD syntax." If you use TDD, the Implement done rule might be, "Code is developed using TDD with BDD naming and validation, it's reviewed, the static analysis is clean, the code is checked in, and the customer-facing documentation is complete."

See also *Chelimsky, David, et al.* The RSpec Book: Behaviour-Driven Development with RSpec, Cucumber, and Friends. *Lewisville, TX: Pragmatic Bookshelf, 2010.*

- **Pair programming**   Pair programming is the practice of two people writing code together. One person, the observer, reviews the code and design as the other person, the driver, types at the keyboard. The driver and observer switch roles several times a day to keep each person fresh, relieve monotony, and maintain a peer relationship. Pair programming keeps individuals engaged, ensures that every line is reviewed, and drives thoughtful conversations about design and implementation choices. In addition to driving focus and code quality, pair programming is also great for information sharing across a team, across disciplines, and with new or inexperienced team members.

  You can leave the use of pair programming up to team members if you want to (relying on healthy peer pressure). If you prefer to ingrain pair programming into your Kanban workflow, you could call your Implement step "Pair program" on your signboard. In addition or instead, you might make your Implement done rule, "Code is pair programmed, the static analysis is clean, the code is checked in, and the customer-facing documentation is complete."

See also *Williams, Laurie, and Robert Kessler.* Pair Programming Illuminated. *Reading, MA: Addison-Wesley, 2002.*

- **DevOps**   DevOps is the practice of developers collaborating closely with service operators to create and maintain software services together. When a service is being designed, service operators directly contribute. When there is a serious production issue, the developer (or developers) who wrote the service that's affected are directly engaged. DevOps is often tied to testing in production (TIP) and continuous deployment.

DevOps can be incorporated into Kanban as described earlier in the "Continuous deployment" section in Chapter 6. In addition, the Validate step may be performed by developers instead of by testers. For a DevOps team, the example of the Validate done rule from the Kanban quick-start guide (Chapter 2) is particularly pertinent: "The work is deployed to production and tried by a significant subset of real customers. All issues found are resolved."

See also *Humble, Jez, and David Farley.* Continuous Delivery: Reliable Software Releases Through Build, Test, and Deployment Automation. *Upper Saddle River, NJ: Addison-Wesley, 2010.*

All of my current and past Xbox teams use DevOps. Many of my teams use TDD and refactoring, and some have used pair programming. All of the methods listed here are valuable and can fit well on your Kanban board.

Why Kanban works

Why does Kanban work so well? It's a combination of visualization, minimalism, Little's Law, single-piece flow, the theory of constraints, and drum-buffer-rope. That's a fair number of concepts, so let's take them up one at a time.

- Visualization is central to Kanban. Everyone can see the signboard, the steps, the done rules, and the work (in the form of note cards) at all times. Visualization provides transparency and easy assessment of status, but more importantly, it provides real-time feedback on the health of your workflow. Other project-management approaches might hide workflow issues until they are bad enough to become self-evident. Kanban visualization brings workflow issues front and center, making them immediately apparent to everyone on the team.

- Minimalism was key to the design of Kanban. Kanban allows teams to keep their existing work-flow processes, roles, responsibilities, and titles. Only minimal adjustments are necessary to adapt Kanban to whatever approach your team prefers yet still enjoy Kanban's substantial pro-ductivity and quality improvements. This makes Kanban easy to use and quick to appreciate.

- Little's Law, a rigorously proven statement from queuing theory, says that the work in prog-ress (WIP) in a system is equal to the average system throughput multiplied by the system response time. Intuitively, the number of items you finish in a day times the number of days it takes to respond to a new item should be the number of items started but not finished.

For software development, the system is the team, its tools, and its processes. That team wants to minimize its response time in order to be competitive in today's technology market-place (that's being agile). Little's Law says response time equals WIP divided by throughput. Therefore, to minimize response time, you've got to reduce WIP and increase through-put. Kanban reduces WIP with its WIP limits and increases throughput by visualizing work (exposing workflow issues), enforcing done rules (which increases quality and reduces rework), and tuning WIP limits to maximize flow.

See also *Reinertsen, Donald.* Managing the Design Factory: A Product Developer's Toolkit. *New York: Free Press, 1997.*

Visualization, minimalism, and Little's Law explain why Kanban works so well at a high level, but tuning WIP limits to maximize flow is worth explaining in more detail. That's where single-piece flow, the theory of constraints, and drum-buffer-rope help determine the right limits.

Single-piece flow

I'll start with an important theoretical statement: the ideal WIP limit is one item, also known as single-piece flow or one-piece flow. That's the smallest WIP you can have, and thus it leads to the fastest-possible response time for a given system throughput. (Zero WIP would mean no work was being done, and fractional WIP would mean no item was entirely completed.)

While single-piece flow is the theoretical ideal, it's rarely achieved in practice. Work varies in size. Work also varies in complexity by step—some work is hardest to specify, some hardest to implement, and some hardest to validate. That variation causes flow issues and can leave people idle. Sometimes having people be idle is good—they can help out folks who are struggling instead of piling on more work. However, switching jobs all the time is taxing and not always helpful. In addition, with a little buffer, the variation can balance out, keeping everyone productive a larger portion of the time (higher throughput). The trick is to make your WIP limits as small as you can, but not so small that there's no buffer. To find the right balance, it's helpful to understand the theory of constraints.

See also *Crenshaw, Dave.* The Myth of Multitasking: How "Doing It All" Gets Nothing Done. *San Francisco: Jossey-Bass, 2008.*

Theory of constraints (TOC)

How do you set your WIP limits to be as small as possible yet keep everyone productive most of the time? Consider a workflow in which all the steps take a day, except for one step, which always takes a week (one person assigned to each step). The fastest throughput you can achieve in this workflow is one item per week. The longest step is a constraint on your throughput.

> **Note** In practice, the longest step can vary by work item, but it helps to think through this simple example first.

Even though the quick steps can produce five items per week (assuming a five-day workweek), the overall throughput remains one item per week (see the following note). If allowed to, the quick steps would just build up an inventory of incomplete work, raising your WIP and thus slowing your response time. (The weeklong step would have to complete the large inventory of pending work before getting to a new item, unless you threw away all the inventory—bad choices.)

> **Note** The quick steps might keep your cycle time short, but they don't impact your throughput. Cycle time is how long it takes for one item to pass through all its steps. However, your team handles more than one item at a time. What matters here is your throughput: that is, how many items your team delivers each day. If your longest step always takes a week, your throughput is always one item per week.

The idea that the longest step acts as a constraint on your throughput is from the theory of constraints (TOC). This theory states that the way to improve throughput is to speed up the longest step, also known as "elevating the constraint." There are several ways to elevate a constraint:

- **Perform the longest step in parallel**   In my example, say you assigned five people to the weeklong step to match the throughput of the other steps. Now you can finish five items per week (five times the throughput). However, the number of items in progress for the long step would go from one to five (five times the WIP). If you had two other steps, each with WIP limits of one, you'd go from a response time of 3 weeks (3 items / 1 item per week) to a response time of 1.4 weeks (7 items / 5 items per week). It's better, but not five times better.

  Adding more than five people to the weeklong step would force you to add more folks to the other steps to keep pace, increasing your WIP and prolonging your response time (see Figure 9-1). The 1.4-week response time is the best you can theoretically achieve, regardless of the number of people you add. It gets the best response time because the throughput of all the steps match (ideal utilization).

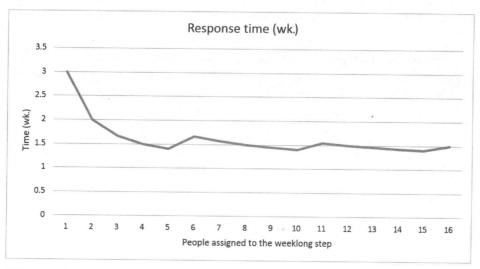

FIGURE 9-1 Response time chart showing time in weeks versus people assigned to the weeklong step.

- **Break down your longest step into smaller steps**   Say you break down the weeklong step into five one-day steps (assuming a five-day workweek). Your throughput goes from one item per week to one item per day, but your WIP for the long step goes from one to five. As before, if you assume two other steps, the response time of 3 weeks would drop to 1.4 weeks (7 items / 1 item per day / 5 days per week). It's definitely better, but this approach involves more people and coordination (though Kanban makes that coordination easier).

- **Change how you do the longest step to make it faster**   This approach is the most effective and has the greatest impact so long as you still achieve the quality bar set by the step's done rule. You can speed up a step through automation, simplification, and thoughtful redesign. Perhaps you're overengineering in places. Perhaps folks spend extra time searching for information, waiting for builds, or being blocked by partners. Anything you can do to make the longest step faster per person will increase your throughput without increasing your WIP, and thus directly improve your response time. In other words, investing in productivity improvements (such as fast build, testing, and deployment) can make a big difference.

TOC provides insight into how you can improve throughput, but it's a particular application of TOC, called "drum-buffer-rope," that solidifies how to balance WIP limits.

> **See also** *Goldratt, Eliyahu M. and Jeff Cox. The Goal: A Process of Ongoing Improvement. 3rd revised edition. Great Barrington, MA: North River Press, 2004.*

Drum-buffer-rope

Regardless of the way you choose to elevate your constraint (your longest step), you never want your longest step to take even longer. Some variation in your longest step is out of your control, but you can control some of it. In particular, there are two mistakes people make that you can avoid:

- **Don't deprive the longest step of work**   Since your throughput depends entirely on your longest step, depriving it of work slows everything down. The longest step should never have to wait.

- **Don't pressure the longest step to be faster**   Actually making the longest step faster is great (you're elevating the constraint), but pressuring people to work faster generally leads to shortcuts, quality issues, and rework. All that rework reduces throughput and increases WIP— the opposite of your goal. (The moral is: respect your done rules.)

Drum-buffer-rope is an application of TOC that avoids both of these mistakes and ensures that the pace of all the steps match to achieve the best response time. As its name signifies, it has three key concepts:

- **Drum**   The drum is the step that takes the longest (the constraint). You need every other step to match the pace of the drum to ensure that the drum is always beating, never overwhelmed, and all steps are fully utilized.

- **Buffer**   The buffer holds extra work items for when the drum varies its pace. You can't avoid variation, particularly in product development. Having a buffer ensures that your drum is always beating.

- **Rope**   The rope limits the shorter steps to produce at the average pace of the drum (the longest step). Having a rope ensures that your drum is never overwhelmed and that all steps are fully utilized.

An adorable drum

David Anderson provided a memorable example of a simple drum-buffer-rope system in his blog. When David would walk his dog, his young daughter liked to join him. David's dog was bigger than his daughter and the fastest of the three of them. No matter what David or the dog did, the length of the walk was determined by David's daughter—she was the constraint.

David used a tether to keep track of his daughter when he needed to collect his dog's output. The tether had enough slack so that his daughter wasn't slowed down. David used a leash to keep the dog in check so that he and the dog kept close to his daughter (letting the dog loose would invite chaos). David's daughter was the drum, the tether was the buffer, and the leash was the rope. As long as David and his dog kept to his daughter's pace, with a little buffer to handle variation, the walk would be delightful.

Applying drum-buffer-rope to Kanban is a bit imperfect because work varies in complexity by step (the same step isn't always the longest). However, one step is typically longest on average, so drum-buffer-rope can provide some insight into balancing WIP limits. Here's another look at the example from the Kanban quick-start guide (Chapter 2), in which the Implement step was the longest on average.

	A	B Specify	C Implement	D Validate	E
1	**Determine WIP Limits**		Fill in cells with yellow highlight		
2					
3	**Step**	**Specify**	**Implement**	**Validate**	
4	A: Average rate per month per person	6	2	3	
5	B: Slowest rate (minimum A column)		2		
6	C: Number of people assigned to step B		3		
7	D: Throughput of step B (B * C)		6		
8	E: People needed to match B's throughput (D / A)	1	3	2	
9	F: WIP limits (E * 1½ rounded up)	2	5	3	

- Because the Implement step is the constraint (the slowest step), it's the drum. We want Implement to always be beating as fast as it can, so we set its WIP limit to be the number of available developers. As I described when discussing TOC, assigning more people to a step can improve response time, particularly if you match the throughput of all the steps (the rope's purpose).

- You need some buffer to hold extra work items for when the pace of the Implement step varies. After all, work items vary in complexity, and developers vary in capability on any given day. I added 50 percent to the Implement WIP limit for use as a buffer. There's no magic to using 50 percent; it's just a starting point that's a big enough proportion to handle variation, yet small enough to not unduly lengthen response time.

- You need some rope to make the Specify and Validate steps match the pace of Implement (its throughput). The pace of each step is its average pace per person times the number of people assigned. The average pace per person for Specify and Validate is fixed, but you can vary the number of people. Set the pace of each step equal to each other, and solve for the number of people. For example, the people assigned to Specify would be the average pace per person for Implement times the number of people assigned to Implement, divided by the average pace per person for Specify. To codify the rope, you set the WIP limit for Specify to be this calculated number of people and do the same for Validate.

- Now you have your drum, buffer, and rope, but you haven't accounted for variation in the pace of Specify and Validate. Remember, work can vary in complexity by step, and the people specifying and validating can vary in capability day by day. Fortunately, Kanban has WIP limits for each step, so you can add buffers to the Specify and Validate WIP limits, as you did for Implement (add 50 percent to each as a starting point). This results in a chain of drum-buffer-rope, with each step limited to match the pace of all the others, and each step has some buffer to manage variation.

Note There may be a fractional number of people needed for the Specify or Validate step (or for both) to match the pace of Implement. That corresponds to folks who need to work on that step only part-time. Instead of leaving you to worry about allocating people, Kanban lets you focus on work. You add 50 percent to the fractional WIP limits for Specify and Validate and round up. This gives you a starting point for WIP limits. The people assigned to Specify and Validate can regulate their time based on available work on the signboard. With WIP limits controlling the flow, no other management is needed.

Kanban's WIP limits control the proper pacing that maintains high utilization and fast response time, including buffers to account for variation across items and steps. You can increase staffing (and corresponding WIP limits) proportionally across all steps to increase throughput while keeping the fast response times. Kanban adds nothing extraneous and achieves the best theoretical and practical results for the steps you already use. That's why Kanban works so well.

See also Cox, James F., and John G. Schleier, eds. Theory of Constraints Handbook. *New York: McGraw-Hill, 2010.*

Improving beyond Kanban

How can you improve beyond Kanban? By reimagining your steps and expanding your worldview.

The evolution from traditional Waterfall to Scrum and to Kanban might give you hope that there's yet another, even better, approach on the horizon. However, Little's Law removes all the magic from differing project-management approaches. It's about WIP and throughput. Kanban takes a direct and minimalist approach to reducing WIP and optimizing throughput. You can find better ways to drive quality up front, incorporate customer feedback, and implement and deploy quality products faster. Those represent important improvements to your steps and done rules. As for controlling WIP and maximizing throughput for those step and done rules, Kanban remains an ideal choice.

How do you improve your steps and done rules?

- **Critical chain**   Break down individual steps and reconfigure them to shorten cycle time and improve throughput.

- **Lean development**   Trim waste, enhance quality, and speed throughput of all your product development steps.

- **Global optimization**   Examine your entire company and industry, viewing the steps you take at a global scale, and consider how those steps could be reengineered for higher quality, lower WIP, and greater throughput.

These improvements represent significant changes to how your business functions. Let's start with the area most under your control: the steps on your Kanban board.

Critical chain

In the theory of constraints (TOC) example earlier in this chapter, all steps took one day on average to complete, except for one step that took five days (the constraint). One approach to elevate that constraint was to break down the step into five one-day steps, which increased WIP but improved throughput. Another approach was to reengineer the long step to make it faster. These two approaches can be used effectively in combination by using the concept of a critical chain.

The critical chain in your workflow is the set of steps that constrain your actual cycle time (given current tooling and staffing). You want to make that chain as short as possible and ensure that it's always active (like the drum in drum-buffer-rope). I talked about how to do that by controlling WIP and matching throughput. You can also do it by reengineering workflow.

Consider a workflow with steps of differing average throughput per person. The steps in dark gray are part of the critical chain that constrain cycle time. I'll break down the steps and reconfigure them.

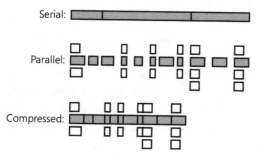

- I start with three serialized steps with the full width (first row) representing the cycle time (the longest step constrains the throughput per person). All three steps are part of the critical chain.

- After breaking down the steps (middle rows), it's evident that some short steps can be done in parallel. The longest of each set of parallel steps are in dark gray because they are the critical chain that governs the cycle time. Note that many of these steps were already being done in parallel (like various kinds of customer engagement and market research). That's why, if you put the short steps end to end, they'd appear longer than the original steps.

- When I put the broken down steps together (last rows), I come up with a compressed cycle time and faster throughput. On a Kanban board, the parallel steps might become separate cards or a change in how the steps are automated or executed (like running buddy builds at the same time as code reviews). The critical chain steps become the steps on the signboard.

Can you improve your new workflow even further? You can by reexamining your workflow steps from a Lean perspective, which I cover in the next section.

See also *Goldratt, Eliyahu M.* Critical Chain. *Great Barrington, MA: North River Press, 1997.*

Lean development

Even after you've reduced your cycle time by applying a critical chain, there is likely a great deal of wasted time and effort in your steps (which is also true if you haven't applied a critical chain). You might sense that waste but have difficulty pinpointing it.

Fortunately, people have been studying wasteful practices in manufacturing for more than a century. Lean manufacturing lists seven different kinds of waste you should avoid. You can adapt these categories to the wide variation in software development and form the basis of Lean development. The categories are:

- **Overproduction** Are you producing more output than necessary? Kanban will prevent you from specifying more than you can implement and from implementing more than you can validate. However, you may still be writing more code than you need, delivering features customers don't use, or producing more artifacts than are required. Are you creating 10-page formal design specs when a photo of a whiteboard would suffice? Are you spending hours creating schedules and estimates when using planning poker and a simple spreadsheet would provide what you require (if anything at all)? Sometimes you need these kinds of additional artifacts that the customer never sees, but often you don't. It's worth reviewing all the work you produce that never reaches the customer, and cutting or simplifying what's unnecessary.

As for writing only the code that you need, there are three philosophies that can help: reuse of existing solutions, "You aren't gonna need it" (YAGNI), and depth-first development. Using existing open source software (OSS) or commercial off-the-shelf (COTS) software and services in areas of undifferentiated value (features everyone has) can save you tremendous effort. (Be sure to carefully follow the OSS licenses.) YAGNI tells you not to create features, interfaces, or extensibility that aren't required right now, because you'll likely not need them or you'll need something different. (TDD fits well with YAGNI.) Do only what's required, and design to accommodate change, not to anticipate change. Depth-first development directs you to complete end-to-end scenarios and stories before starting new ones (like Kanban does for features and tasks, but with wider scope). It's like developing a video game one room or level at a time instead of writing the architectural components separately. With depth-first development, you avoid creating more than you need and also benefit from frequent customer feedback.

- **Transportation**   Are you spending excess time moving information from one place to another? Examples include steps that rely on email messages, file copies, builds, deployments, or branch integrations. Look for ways to speed up this information transfer, like team instant messaging, automation, faster build and deployment systems, and shallower branching to reduce integrations.

- **Motion**   Do you spend too much time searching for existing information? Reducing that wasted motion will speed up your work. A little information organization can go a long way. (My teams are particularly fond of OneNote.) Another common example of wasted searching is debugging. Typically, the earlier you find bugs, the faster you can fix them because all the information is still fresh in your mind and you've made fewer changes that might have caused the issue. Code reviews and TDD can help.

- **Waiting**   Are tasks often waiting for dependencies? Kanban helps a great deal with ordering work and providing it just in time. However, stable or late dependencies can often make you late. That subject is covered in Chapter 7, "Using Kanban within large organizations."

- **Overprocessing**   Are you required to do more work than necessary? Some teams can be sticklers for style, variable and function naming, commenting, long and detailed specifications, mocks, fakes, and unit testing. These are all good practices that have value, but they can all be overdone. Be pragmatic and do as much as needed for customer quality, but no more. When in doubt, try using static analysis to catch issues, be a little more flexible, and then clamp down should customer quality suffer.

- **Inventory**   Do you have more work in progress than necessary? Kanban nicely limits WIP, but you can often do more. Breaking down steps is a good exercise to find problems and opportunities, but doing this need not be permanent. Splitting steps can add to WIP, transportation, motion, and waiting, so only leave steps split if it's helping you significantly with throughput or removing other waste.

- **Defects**   Does your approach and environment lead to bugs? Kanban does a great deal to drive quality at every step with its done rules and continuous customer feedback. However, defects can happen anywhere and everywhere. Your email communication can be defective, leading to miscommunication and rework. Your tools and processes can have defects that force rework, rebuilds, and redeployments. You should have an eye toward quality for everything you do. Every pattern of defects should receive a root-cause analysis and have its root cause corrected. Continuous improvement (kaizen) is the goal in all things because its return on investment is so high.

These seven forms of waste for Lean development require constant vigilance. Learn to spot them and fix them as part of your continuous improvement efforts.

See also *Poppendieck, Mary, and Tom Poppendieck.* Lean Software Development: An Agile Toolkit. *Upper Saddle River, NJ: Addison-Wesley, 2003.*

Global optimization

Some people associate Lean thinking with cutting back on excesses and achieving efficiency for specific tasks. However, real Lean thinking is about delivering the greatest value to customers with the least amount of time, effort, and cost. Value to customers is primary. For example, Scenario-Focused Engineering (SFE) relies heavily on prototypes and design iterations that you throw away. Is that wasted effort? Not if it brings you greater customer value faster.

SFE is an example of striving to build the right product, not just to build the product right. When you locally optimize your team's efforts, you might do some parts well, but you'll achieve limited success. When you globally optimize your entire company's efforts, you'll achieve tremendous customer value as well as high profits and low costs. Global optimization brings broad benefits, but it requires extensive (sometimes industrywide) collaboration and change. It's difficult, but it's game changing when possible.

To globally optimize your company's delivery of customer value, you need to deeply understand your customers and the value they want to receive. You must rely on more than what they say. You must also rely on what they do. (SFE addresses this in detail.) With online services, many companies learn about what their customers do from instrumentation and online experimentation (like A/B testing). But what do you instrument and what do you test?

The secret to global optimization is following the value your customers seek from the time it is demanded to the time it is delivered. As an example, consider a doctor's office. The value customers seek when visiting a doctor's office is to be well again. To globally optimize a doctor's office, you seek to deliver the greatest customer value (wellness) with the least amount of time, effort, and cost. Thus, the things to instrument and test include the following:

- How long does it take from the time a person contacts a doctor's office with an illness or injury until the time they are well again? (The cycle time.)

- How many patient and staff hours are spent getting the person well again? (The effort required.)

- How much money is spent in equipment usage and external services getting the person well again? (The cost incurred.)

Note The cycle time isn't the time spent during the office visit. That would be a local optimization. We are interested in global optimization, so we count the time, effort, and cost from the initial demand for value (the first contact with the doctor's office) to the value delivery (the patient is well again).

Since you want to minimize time, effort, and cost, you need to understand what generates each and how they may be wasted. I covered waste earlier in the discussion of Lean development. There are two major generators of time, effort, and cost: value demand (the patient's first contact) and failure demand (subsequent contacts as the result of continued illness). You desire value demand—it's the source of your business. You disparage failure demand and all forms of waste.

To achieve the goal of minimizing failure demand and all forms of waste, you need to consider the value stream: the workflow that takes you from value demand (initial patient contact) to value delivery (patient wellness). A typical patient workflow in the United States might look like Figure 9-2.

FIGURE 9-2 Twenty-two steps a patient in the United States might commonly take to regain health.

- The patient calls a doctor's office, complains of an ailment, and arranges a future office visit.

- On the appointment day, the patient drives to the office, presents identification and proof of insurance at the front desk, updates contact and health information, and waits to be seen.

- A nurse gathers the patient, collects vitals (height, weight, blood pressure, pulse, and temperature), and notes what's troubling the patient.

- The patient waits in an exam room for the doctor.

- The doctor arrives, reviews the notes, examines the patient, and discusses the ailment. At this point, the doctor may refer the patient to a specialist, in which case all these steps repeat.

- Once the doctor or specialist arrives at a diagnosis, the physician describes treatment options and prescribes follow-on medicines, tests, and treatment.

- The patient acquires medicines from a pharmacy (another significant process).

- If there are tests or treatment, the patient repeats most (and often all) of these steps associated with the doctor visit until fully recovered. (I don't show those steps in the diagram.)

- The patient is healthy again.

An initial review of the value stream highlights several sources of failure demand and waste. These deficiencies are addressed in the workflow shown in Figure 9-3, which illustrates what a globally optimized workflow might look like.

Drive to doctor   Nurse collects vitals and info   Doctor exam   Doctor and specialist consultation   Recieve medicine   Healthy

FIGURE 9-3 Six globally optimized steps a patient might take to regain health.

- There's waiting between the initial call and the office visit. The office should be staffed sufficiently to handle value demand so that patients can visit without an appointment. The potential underutilization of staff can be covered in other ways, but even if it wasn't, you'd still have lower costs per patient as a result of higher throughput and shorter cycle time.

- Arrival at the office is full of overprocessing, excess motion, inventory, and waiting, all of which is repeated when a patient sees a specialist. There are political and privacy issues with tying online medical information to identification cards nationally, but there's nothing that prevents an individual doctor's office or collective from providing this convenience online and having the information available when you arrive.

- Collecting vitals and other basic information as well as the ensuing wait for a doctor have issues with excess motion, waiting, and inventory. Many pharmacies have automated chairs that can take your vitals while you wait for a prescription. Imagine having one or two slightly more sophisticated versions of these chairs at a doctor's office. When you arrive at the office, a nurse guides you into one of the chairs. You present your identification to the chair (the nurse can help patients who are confused or incapacitated). The chair notifies an available doctor of your presence. As the chair measures your height, weight, blood pressure, pulse, and temperature, the nurse collects information about your ailment. By the time the chair finishes taking your vital signs, the doctor has come to escort you to an exam room.

- The diagnosis, pharmacy, and follow-on tests and treatments contain substantial issues with failure demand and overproduction, transportation, motion, waiting, overprocessing, inventory, and defects (all seven kinds of waste). Having a separate interaction at the pharmacy is a problem, but the primary driver of cycle time (time to wellness) is proper diagnosis and timely treatment, which in turn is tied to bringing the right expertise to the patient in a timely fashion.

  Imagine that the doctor had the option of engaging an expert system and a broad collection of specialists via online consultation. For straightforward cases, the doctor could provide you the diagnosis and treatment plan immediately (optionally, with assistance from the expert system). For cases referred to a specialist, two specialists would instantly connect with you and your doctor online. The specialists would ask you and your doctor questions and discuss the case. Two specialist opinions, in the presence of you and your doctor, would significantly improve the accuracy of your diagnosis (fewer defects), the focus of testing (less overproduction), and the effectiveness of the treatment plan (less failure demand)—as second opinions do today, but without the waste created by waiting, motion, transportation, or inventory. Any necessary follow-on visits for testing or specialist care would be scheduled before you leave, with your health data transmitted in advance by your consent.

- The doctor's office could locate itself near a pharmacy with which it has an agreement. In return for preferred business, the pharmacy would deliver prescriptions directly to the doctor's office within 10 minutes of electronic ordering. As soon as the doctor (or specialists) decide on a treatment plan, the system orders any prescriptions. By the time your doctor has described the treatment plan and you've gotten dressed, your medicines arrive and you can begin treatment. (Many hospital pharmacies function this way today.)

The globally optimized value stream for treating ailments assumes that a doctor's office has enough staff to handle demand and that two specialists are immediately available online to help diagnose any kind of ailment. (There are also assumptions about chairs, online systems, pharmacies, and expert systems, but those aren't as much of a stretch.) The staffing assumptions may seem extravagant (not lean at all). However, failure demand and waste are dramatically reduced in the optimized value stream. This frees up time to focus on value demand.

In the optimized value stream, doctors are kept busy with patients in their office or are helping other doctors online. Even if doctors are occasionally idle because of variation in value demand (as they are today), the substantial savings (not to mention delighted patients) would more than pay for the difference. Customers get better faster, with less effort, at lower cost. That permits the doctor's office to treat more customers with fewer staff in less time.

Global optimization leads to unusual-sounding results. The idea that you could feel ill, drive to your doctor's office, walk through the door right to a chair, sit for a minute while a nurse notes your ailment, have your doctor arrive as you get up, receive an accurate diagnosis and effective treatment plan at the same visit (possibly from two specialists), and be handed your medicine by the time you're dressed is astonishing. That such a value stream would be more profitable is even more astonishing.

Why doesn't global optimization, like the one described in the doctor's office example, happen more frequently? Because our society's systems develop over time. As they develop, people naturally optimize their systems locally (the ones around them), not globally. This book is no different—the first eight chapters are about local optimization. Optimizing systems globally often requires broad and dramatic change, which usually isn't practical. However, if you're willing and able, global optimization is well worth the effort.

See also Seddon, John. Freedom from Command and Control: A Better Way to Make the Work Work. *Vanguard Education, 2005.*

See also Womack, James P., and Daniel T. Jones. Lean Thinking: Banish Waste and Create Wealth in Your Corporation. *New York: Free Press, 2003.*

See also Modig, Niklas, and Pär Åhlström. This Is Lean: Resolving the Efficiency Paradox. *Rheologica, 2012.*

Checklist

Here's a checklist of actions to learn more and go beyond Kanban:

- ❑ Add separate swim lanes for different types of work items that go through different workflows.

- ❑ As needed, expand your Kanban board to include steps prior to specification (such as customer research) and after validation (such as feature delivery).

- ❑ Use Personal Kanban to organize your to-do list and focus your efforts.

- ❑ Enhance your agility with test-driven development (TDD), refactoring, acceptance test-driven development (ATDD), behavior-driven development (BDD), pair programming, or DevOps.

- ❑ Learn about how Kanban works by studying Little's Law, single-piece flow, the theory of constraints (TOC), and drum-buffer-rope.

- ❑ Apply a critical chain to break down individual steps and reconfigure them in ways that shorten cycle time and improve throughput.

- ❑ Trim waste, enhance quality, and speed throughput of all your product development steps with Lean thinking.

- ❑ Globally optimize your entire company's value stream to improve quality, lower costs, and increase productivity.

- ❑ Read further about your favorite advanced project-management topics in the books I listed in this chapter.

Index

About the author

Eric Brechner is the development manager for the Xbox Engineering Services team. He is widely known within the engineering community as his alter ego, I. M. Wright. Prior to his current assignment, Eric managed development for the Xbox.com websites, was director of engineering learning and development for Microsoft Corporation, and managed development for a shared feature team in Microsoft Office. Before joining Microsoft in 1995, he was a senior principal scientist at Boeing and a developer for Silicon Graphics, Graftek, and JPL. Eric has published a book on software best practices and holds eight patents, a BS and MS in mathematics, and a PhD in applied mathematics. He is an affiliate professor evenings at the University of Washington's Bothell campus.

Now that you've read the book...

Tell us what you think!

Was it useful?
Did it teach you what you wanted to learn?
Was there room for improvement?

Let us know at http://aka.ms/tellpress

Your feedback goes directly to the staff at Microsoft Press,
and we read every one of your responses. Thanks in advance!

 Microsoft